The Springer Series on Death and Suicide
ROBERT KASTENBAUM, Ph.D., Series Editor

SUICIDE AFTER SIXTY
The Final Alternative

MARV MILLER, *Ph.D.*

SPRINGER PUBLISHING COMPANY
New York

Copyright © 1979 by Marv Miller, Ph.D.

Springer Publishing Company, Inc.
200 Park Avenue South
New York, N.Y. 10003

Author's note: Sections of this book, principally chapters 12, 13, and 14, have been previously published under the titles "The Physician and the Older Suicidal Patient" (*The Journal of Family Practice* 5:1028–1029, December 1977), "A Psychological Autopsy of a Geriatric Suicide" (*The Journal of Geriatric Psychiatry* 10:229–242, March 1978), "Geriatric Suicide: The Arizona Study" (*The Gerontologist* 18:488–495, October 1978), and "Cooperation of Some Wives in Their Husbands' Suicides" (Psychological Reports 44:39–42, February 1979).

83 / 10 9 8 7 6 5 4 3 2

Library of Congress Cataloging in Publication Data

Miller, Marv.
  Suicide after sixty.

  (Springer series on death and suicide; v. 2)
  Bibliography: p.
  Includes index.
  1. Suicide. 2. Geriatric psychiatry. I. Title.
II. Series.
RC569.M54   618.9'76'85844   79-4246
ISBN 0-8261-2780-0
ISBN 0-8261-2781-9 pbk.

Printed in the United States of America

In memory of Albert Miller

Contents

1

An Introduction to the Problem

Older Americans are deadly serious about killing themselves. People 60 and older represent 18.5 percent of the United States population, but commit 23.0 percent of all suicides;* yet the stereotypical view of suicide as primarily a problem of the young persists. The phenomenon of geriatric suicide is certainly not peculiar to the United States. On the contrary, a pattern of suicide rates increasing with age may be observed in almost every country where suicide statistics are maintained.[16,53]

In relation to the size of other age groups in the United States, each year the elderly commit suicide the most, but attempt suicide the least.[22] Older people also tend to communicate their suicidal intentions less frequently, to use lethal weapons more often, and to be more successful in killing themselves than the young.[10,34,47] Unlike many younger people, the aged do not often use suicidal activities as a means of manipulating others, calling attention to themselves, or crying out for help.[15,16] Older

*SOURCE: 1975 data from The National Center for Health Statistics. People less than 10 years old are excluded from the agency's suicide statistics.

people contemplating suicide also tend to be much less ambivalent than the young and are therefore less likely to be rescued from their suicidal activities.[46,47,133]

The Underreporting of Suicides

A remarkably large number of suicides are never reported as such. Most experts agree the number of suicides that are falsely certified as accidents or natural deaths in the United States each year may be as great as the number of reported suicides. A few of the numerous reasons for the underreporting are: (1) not wanting to stigmatize the surviving family; (2) allowing the survivors to collect larger amounts of life insurance benefits; (3) families that destroy or hide suicide notes; and (4) coroners only certifying a suicide when a note has been found (even though research has shown the majority of suicides don't leave notes). It seems reasonable to assume the underreporting of suicidal deaths occurs even more often among the elderly because the certification of an older person's death as accidental or natural would not normally arouse much curiosity.

The author estimates at least 10,000 people 60 and older kill themselves in our country each year. In 1975 there were 27,063 certified suicides nationally. Of those, 6,228 were reported as having been committed by people 60 and older. When the notorious underreporting of suicides is taken into account, the 10,000-person estimate may actually be conservative.

A Brief Historical View

During 1950–1970 there was a noticeable decline in geriatric suicide rates in the United States. For example, the rate for white males aged 65–74 dropped 26 percent. There was also a similar decline in England, Norway, and Denmark. Some suicidologists attributed the decrease to broader social security coverage and increased benefits.[106] Others felt there were numerous variables involved,[47] since a British study indicated high suicide rates among the aged were not related to the economic assistance provided by various old age pension systems.[51] However, it is important to realize there has still been a continuous increase in the number of aged people and in the number of their suicides.[47]

A statistical study of suicide in England concluded: "Suicide in the last 50 years has increasingly become a disorder of elderly people . . . as the present century has advanced, the old may have found their environment more hostile than the young."[139]

Male versus Female Suicides

Suicidologists have known since the turn of the century that men complete suicide three times as often as women, but women attempt suicide three times as often as men.[13,97,105] Because suicides among women have been increasing, the male/female ratio is gradually shrinking. However, the disparity of male and female suicide rates becomes much more dramatic in late life. During ages 65–69, male suicides outnumber their female counterparts by a four to one ratio. By 85 this ratio increases to about twelve to one.[13,46,58] The suicide rate for older white males is almost four times greater than the average rate for the United States as a whole.[15,47,133] The predominance of male geriatric suicides may be observed in Figure 1.

While the suicide rate for the United States has remained between 9 and 13 per 100,000 since World War II, the rate for older white males has ranged between 40/100,000 and 75/100,000.[104] The suicide rate for women tends to reach its peak by or before 55, while for men, the rate continues to increase steadily through the eighth decade of life.[9,12,13,53]

There is still no satisfactory explanation of why suicide is more common among men. Depression, the mental state most frequently associated with successful suicide in old age, is at least

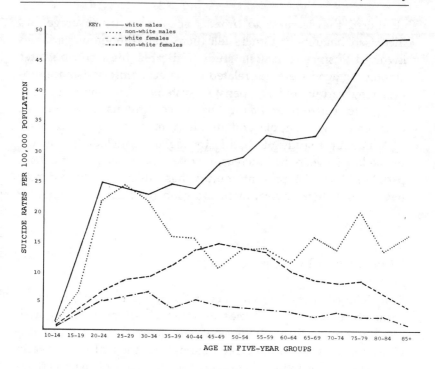

Source: The National Center for Health Statistics

Figure 1. Suicide Rates in the United States in Relation to Age and Race (1974)

as common among women. Perhaps the impact of retirement and physical decline is more devastating to the self-esteem of men than women in today's society.[15]

White versus Nonwhite Suicides

The suicide rate for nonwhites is generally lower than the rate for whites.[15] Although the suicide rates for American Indians[102] and blacks[58,111,112] aged 15 through 29 may be higher than what they are for whites at those ages, it is only among white males that the suicide rate increases throughout the life cycle.

Some researchers surmise the extreme plurality of white male suicides in later life is due to the severe loss of status that affects white men so much more drastically than blacks. As they grow older, white men often lose their power and influence, whereas black men and women have long been accustomed to a lower status because of racism and sexism. Therefore, members of these minorities do not have to suffer such losses in old age. In fact, there are indications black people in our country actually experience an increase in social status as they age.[16]

Suicide and Religion

Of the three major religious groups in the United States, Jews appear to have the lowest suicide rates; Catholic rates are higher and Protestants consistently have the highest rates of all. Whenever one considers suicide statistics, particularly in relation to religion, it is important to bear in mind how difficult they are to compile. For instance, think of the difficulty in precisely defining what is a Jew, a Catholic, or a Protestant.

So many civilizations have tried to kill the Jews throughout history that the net effect may have been to make life seem more precious to them by emphasizing sheer survival. A similar effect is seen during international warfare when suicide rates decline. There are also strong family ties among many Jews, and what Durkheim called "strong social integration."[102] However, the suicide rates among Jews in Israel and certain other parts of the world are beginning to increase.

The Catholic Church brings a strong sense of integration into people's lives, with its tightly knit order and its authoritarian body of common beliefs and dogmas. The Church also teaches suicide is a mortal sin that is punishable in the hereafter. These factors seem to have exerted a definitely inhibiting effect on the suicide rate for Catholics in general, yet certain predominantly

Catholic countries such as Austria consistently have high suicide rates.

The highest suicide rates are those of the loosely federated Protestants. With its numerous factions, it may be much more difficult for the Protestant Church to "speak with one voice," and the resultant lack of uniformity may therefore hamper group identification and integration. High suicide rates among Protestants were documented as early as 1897.[105]

Understanding Geriatric Suicides

Why has the unnecessary tragedy of geriatric suicides in the United States been allowed to continue unchecked? The primary reason is that suicide is such a complex behavior it is exceptionally difficult to prevent or effectively control. For example, a host of psychological instruments have been used to try to predict suicide risk, but so far they have only produced an unacceptably high number of "false positives" (people who appear to be potentially suicidal on paper, but who aren't so in reality). And as frustrated behavioral scientists retreat to their drawing boards, the number of suicides continues to rise each year.

Another basic reason is that a very low priority seems to be placed on saving the lives of those who have left the work force. After people retire in the United States, their status usually diminishes because they are no longer productive in an economic sense. Therefore, the deaths of such people do not represent a serious loss to the economy. Because it is also felt "older people have already had a chance to live their lives, while younger people have not," saving the lives of suicidal adolescents and young adults has traditionally been the major focus of much of the suicide prevention, intervention, and research efforts.

A third reason is that many geriatric suicides involve both suicide and euthanasia and even people who are adamantly opposed to suicide per se are often able to condone it when the purpose is to relieve pain, suffering, and extreme anguish.

The Complexity of Geriatric Suicides

No one factor in any person's life is in itself suicidogenic. Indeed, there appear to be as many distinct clusters of variables as there are older people who kill themselves. *The crucial factor seems to be how well developed and efficacious are the person's coping abilities.* In other words, it isn't any given trauma that precipitates the suicidal episode, but rather the older person's reaction to the predicament. For example, some people experience grave tragedies in their later years, but never even think of committing suicide. Conversely, other people lose their desire to live because they develop various fears.[35]

Suicidal behavior is often associated with an inability to cope with vital losses. Obviously, the older a person is, the longer time there has been in which to have suffered significant losses. That is not to say a 20-year-old married man could not suddenly become a widower while his 80-year-old grandfather's first marriage is still intact. But, generally, the older a person is, the more losses he will have incurred. Also, younger people are more likely to replace their losses. Most 20-year-old widowers will remarry, as will most 20-year-old divorcees; however, the chances of someone 60 or older remarrying are only about one in six.

Vital losses may be quite diverse, but what they all have in common is their deleterious effect. Such losses may be *economic* (loss of a job or income); *physical* (loss of a limb or good health); *social* (loss of a best friend or a cherished neighborhood); *psychological* (loss of self-esteem or confidence); *emotional* (loss of a spouse or a child); or any combination thereof. *What is important is not any one loss in particular, but the unexpectedness and swiftness of its occurrence, the sufferer's reaction to it, and its synergistic effect when combined with extant problems.* That is why a rapid succession of losses can be so devastating.

Why then do only a small minority of the older people plagued with multiple losses and problems actually commit suicide? Perhaps the answer is that many older people have developed remarkably resilient personalities that enable them to cope successfully with virtually any trauma. Having learned how important it is to try to supplant their vital losses rather than dwell on them, their positive approach to life becomes a buffer that insulates them from suicide. Other less fortunate older people who never developed similar abilities may live a highly tentative, marginal existence while merely trying to survive. Add a few negatives to their already dismal lives and they will kill themselves without hesitation.

There is also the essential distinction between the "quality of life" and the "quantity of life." Lying dormant within all of us is an extremely personal equation which determines the point where the quality of our lives would be so pathetically poor we would no longer wish to live. This "line of unbearability," as it might be called, usually exists only subconsciously and we are therefore not normally cognizant of it. However, when we actually find ourselves in an intolerable situation, even for the first time in our lives, we become conscious of our "line of unbearability."

Once the line of unbearability is crossed, a crisis is triggered. Those who still maintain hope cry out for help. Those who don't are likely to kill themselves quickly and with determination. (NOTE: For a detailed explanation of suicide as a function of hope, see reference 106.) The real tragedy is that most of those people could probably cope successfully with any one of their problems if only each problem could be isolated long enough to be treated by itself. However, as indicated, when problems strike en masse, or are simply added to a nexus of unresolved problems, the result may be suicide. To make matters much more difficult, the majority of older people who become suicidal have never been that way before and therefore cannot rely on their experience to help them.

What would cause a person to cross his line of unbearability? Because the perception of what constitutes an unbearable plight is so extremely personal, no two people's constellation of problems is identical. A good example concerns the people who kill themselves because they suspect they have cancer. Although several doctors may have assured them of their good health, the mere spectre of cancer may push them to the point where they will kill themselves rather than continue living with their dread.

On the other hand, many people who actually die of cancer never even consider taking their lives.

Another example is widowerhood. After some wives die, their husbands kill themselves rather than try to cope with their grief, yet other widowers outlive two or three wives and still don't kill themselves. Therefore, it seems reasonable to conclude *the salient variables in these life-versus-death considerations are: (1) how well developed the individual's coping abilities are, and (2) how strong the "will to live" is.*

In some cases, the problems that seriously detract from the quality of the lives of people who commit suicide appear to be caused by emotional vestiges of childhood situations which have continued to torment them throughout their lives. In these cases, the most important etiological factor seems to be an extremely domineering parent who was insensitive, inconsiderate, and possibly violent. Because of the detrimental influence of such parents, many people appear to have already been pointed in a suicidal direction while still children. A classic example is an 8-year-old boy who was forced to watch his alcoholic father beat his dog to death. This brutal event so traumatized the boy, he continued to recall its agony and cry about it for the next 60 years. While still a child he ran away from home and had continued running from every troublesome situation he faced during the remainder of his life. The boy grew up to become an alcoholic like his father and eventually killed himself (see Case Twelve).

2

A Review of the Literature on Geriatric Suicide

In order to provide further background and a broader perspective of the problem, the literature related to suicide among the elderly will be reviewed, under the following headings: (1) Familial and Personal Histories; (2) Mental and Emotional Problems; (3) Physical Illness and Symptomatology; (4) Social Factors; (5) Precipitating Factors and Motives; (6) Means of Lethality; (7) Prevention; and (8) Intervention.

These categories overlap considerably. For instance, the traumatic effect retirement has on some older people relates not only to the topics of "Social Factors" and "Precipitating Factors and Motives," but also to "Prevention."

Familial and Personal Histories

Suicide victims and attempters appear to have a greater number of unfavorable factors in their histories than do people who are not suicidal. These negative factors include family members that have been institutionalized for mental illness, broken homes in childhood, and prior indications of depression.[9]

In a follow-up study of 40 suicide attempts by people 60 and older in Scotland, a family history of suicidal acts was noted in 17 percent of the cases and psychiatric abnormalities were found in the majority of the families.[5] A familial manic-depressive trait appears to have been a common thread running through numerous cases of geriatric suicides studied in Scotland.

Even the suicidal elderly who have not previously been mentally ill often show personality traits which limit social adaptation (undue sensitivity, shyness, dependency, egocentricity, restricted interests, anxiety, and hypochondriasis).[4] In half of the 40 cases in the Scottish study, social adaptation was considered defective: the individuals lived outside of social groups and had few friends.[5] In fact, a quarter of the suicide attempters in Scotland were men and women who had never married. However, further investigation into the backgrounds of older suicides is in order because a study in St. Louis showed there was little or nothing exceptional in the personal histories of geriatric suicidal patients.[43]

Mental and Emotional Problems

In the opinion of one researcher, "The most important determining factor for suicide in old age is the mental illness from which the old person is usually suffering."[4] He felt the great majority of suicidal elderly suffer from psychoses that are either organic dementias or one of the depressive states, while a minority suffer from the typical organic psychoses such as cerebral arteriosclerosis or senile dementia.[4] In two studies of attempted suicides of people 60 and older, it was found that 26 percent of one group[43] and 10 percent of another[5] were included in the latter categories.

It is likely that all suicidal people are depressed.[4,16] Such depressions include not only psychotic depression or the depression associated with lucid moments of the cerebral arteriosclerotic patient, but also those resulting from loss, grief, and despair.[13]

Depression will also frequently follow physical illnesses, including viral infections and sometimes Parkinson's disease.[16] Varying
degrees of depression may also be found when self-esteem has
been diminished to reduced social and personal status.

A small number of older people appear to attempt suicide
when confused. This confusion is usually of acute onset, is tran-
sient, and is most often organically determined (for example, a
delirium due to intoxication, cerebral anemia, metabolic disorder, or vitamin deficiency). In isolated cases the confusion may
be psychogenic, such as a sudden reaction of panic that leads to
disorientation and a clouding of consciousness.[4]

The psychiatric diagnoses of elderly people who attempt suicide are similar to the diagnoses of those who actually commit
suicide,[15] but the same is not true of the young. The higher
frequency of serious suicide attempts among older rather than
younger people appears to be related to two factors: (1) serious
suicide attempts occur more frequently in patients with manic-
depressive psychosis and chronic brain syndrome than in other
psychiatric illnesses, and (2) these diseases occur more frequently
in older people.[43]

Some elderly suicidal people experience delusions of poverty
and fears of being alone, having a fatal illness, or becoming insane. The mere threat of admission to a mental hospital will
sometimes trigger a suicidal episode.[35]

Although men face an increased risk of suicide with age, older
men are less likely to seek or receive psychiatric care than other
groups with a much lower suicidal risk.[21] There is also an indication some clinicians are disinclined to treat such patients because
they represent low status and/or a poor investment of time.[21,114]

Physical Illness and Symptomatology

Physical illness is frequently a contributory factor to suicide in
late life.[13,35] However, one researcher felt physical illness is not
the precipitating factor in the majority of older suicides, even

though degenerative diseases are commonly found in that age group.[4] He did acknowledge nervous diseases directly diminish control over behavior, while other illnesses may also weaken inhibitions by causing fatigue and lowering an older person's general resistance to stress. Physical illness may also cause brooding, introspection, and may eventually bring the older person to a harsh realization of his frailty or the threat of permanent invalidism and dependency.

Physical infirmity, chronic illness, or the diagnosis of an incurable disease often leads older people to depression and suicidal episodes.[9] An explanation for this phenomenon may be that the older person has greater difficulty in evolving new values and a self-image that can tolerate and incorporate infirmity.[9] Such an adjustment appears to be unusually difficult for older men to achieve and the inability to achieve it may predispose some of them to suicide. For example, many older suicide attempters have reported they were greatly distressed when they first "felt their age," or "felt done."[4] It seems the more abruptly this inimical self-awareness comes about, the more likely it is to be intolerable.

What are the salient symptoms of the suicidal elderly? Depression, insomnia, tension, and agitation are nearly always present. If hypochondriacal bodily complaints are expressed, they tend to be focused on the head and alimentary tract, and are often delusional.[4] For example, an older person may complain his head or abdomen will burst as a result of internal pressure.

Social Factors

Suicide completers tend to be old, married males who have lived successful and independent lives, but who are in poor health and socially isolated.[12] Other characteristics of people who commit suicide in late life are: lack of employment; alcohol abuse; and solitary living arrangements, especially in the deteriorating central sections of the city.[15,21]

The highest suicide rates are found among men who are divorced, followed by the widowed, and those who have never married. Although the lowest rates are for people whose marriages are intact,[15] the overwhelming majority of people who commit suicide are married. This is simply because most adults are married. In other words, although the suicide *rate* for the married is low, in terms of *absolute numbers* many more suicides are married than not married.

Another indication that being married per se will not prevent suicide was the study indicating that elderly spouses who depend solely on their marriages appear more likely to commit suicide than the widowed who are engaged in a network of kin relationships and other types of community interactions.[10]

Among people who are married, children appear to be a buffer against suicide. Research indicates suicide decreases as each of the first five children is added to a family.[54]

The widowed represent a population at considerable risk of suicide.[21,24,33,132] This may occur not only because they are widowed, but also because they are isolated in several other respects (from relatives, friends, neighbors, and community organizations). Many widowed people live alone, and suicide rates are higher for older people who live alone.[21,47] In a study of suicide in London, 39 percent of the suicides aged 60 and older were living alone, a significantly larger proportion than for the middle-aged (23 percent) or younger suicides (16 percent).[51,54]

The impact of widowhood on the elderly and its significance for suicide may still not be as great as retirement, because it is retirement that removes a person from significant sources of self-identity—the occupational role and interaction with friends and coworkers.[10]

Retirement may also be related to the decrease of geriatric suicides in the higher social classes and the increase in the lower classes. It has been suggested that members of the higher classes retire to more secure economic situations than those of the lower classes. However, this may not be the critical factor because the higher classes also tend to retire to opportunities for more varied interests and outlets.[51] Perhaps these are the factors that help to insulate the upper class aged from suicide.

Although people who are married have the lowest overall suicide rate of any of the marital statuses, even their rate shows a distinct rise after age 60 and it appears likely this phenomenon is also related to retirement.[63]

Aging after retirement is mostly a "gearing-down" process closely identified with declines in status, income, power, years remaining to live, roles, physical and mental health, numbers of friends and relatives, usefulness, identity, self-esteem, independence, social and physical mobility, concern of the community, security, hope, and realistic options for solving personal problems.[46] Any combination of these declines may be suicidogenic for an older person.

Remaining gainfully employed seems to be a vital factor inhibiting suicidal behavior among the elderly. Especially for the older male, being employed means one has a purpose to one's activities, one is fulfilling a valued social function, and is a useful member of the community.[5] To be unoccupied is to become isolated from society, which in turn engenders anomic and egoistic suicides.

Adverse social factors of a material nature have been found not to be as closely related to suicide as community attitudes, especially those that tend to make the older person feel useless and unwanted.[5] The elderly who have lost much in social status appear to be more likely to commit suicide than those who have always been used to having little.[4]

Precipitating Factors and Motives

In old age, suicide is rarely an immediate response to a simple frustration. Consequently, precipitating factors and motives tend to be much more subtle and less easily identifiable than they are with young people.[4] While many more young people attempt rather than complete suicide—the ratio has been estimated to be 50 to 1—most older people who attempt suicide actually succeed in killing themselves.[5,43,104] When an older person becomes suicidal, there is usually a strong intent to die. Therefore, rescue from a suicidal episode in late life is often accidental or merely due to poor planning.[15]

The final precipitating factor may be a crisis during which the older person who does not belong to any groups is deprived of the community's emotional support. Such a crisis is often caused by the death of close friends and relatives, loss of employment, economic insecurity, and feelings of rejection and uselessness.[22]

In a group of suicidal people 60 and older in Scotland, feelings of loneliness, of being a burden to others, or of being unwanted were found in 23 of 40 cases.[5] On the other hand, a group of researchers in St. Louis found only 3 of 19 subjects gave loneliness as a reason for their suicide attempts, and in each of those cases the loneliness had resulted from the death of a loved one.[43] The actual importance of loneliness is, therefore, a factor which requires further investigation.

Only a minority of the people who call the Los Angeles Suicide Prevention Center for assistance are elderly. However, many of the aged who do call are lonely, distressed, experiencing physical pain, and angry because they feel deserted. Many of the older male callers are still concerned with sexual satisfaction and feel rejected and frustrated because their wives or girlfriends are not responsive enough.[17]

There is little doubt that loss of loved ones heightens suicidal potential among the aged.[47] One study noted how the loss or death of close friends in the later years had occurred twice as often among a group of suicide attempters than it had among a control group.[123] Changes of home and neighborhood coupled with removal from friends and association are often poorly tolerated in old age.

Research has consistently shown there is a high incidence of alcohol abuse among the suicidal elderly.[25] By releasing inhibitions, the ingestion of alcohol will sometimes lead to a suicide attempt in late life by someone who may not have previously used alcohol excessively.[15] A study of suicide and psychiatric care among the elderly in Monroe County, New York, found that 17 percent of the older suicides with known psychiatric contact had a history of alcoholism.[21]

Excessive use of alcohol appears to function as a means of dulling feelings of bitterness and relieving the anguish produced by being alone. Studies at the Los Angeles Suicide Prevention Center determined alcohol abuse was not uncommon among older women, although it was certainly more common among older men.[17]

The need to have control is another motivational element sometimes present in geriatric suicidal episodes. Death itself is certain enough, but its timing and character are not. The motivation to defy and control death to some degree seems to encourage some older people to kill themselves rather than wait passively for death to overtake them.[16,22] Control also extends beyond the grave; survivors of those who commit suicide may be deeply affected by the legacy of guilt, shame, and regret which the suicide has left for them.

The melange of possible factors precipitating geriatric suicide was illustrated by a study of 19 older people who attempted suicide in St. Louis.[43] Eight of the people indicated depressed feelings; 4 experienced depressive delusions; 1 did not remember the attempt (because of amnesia associated with a senile psychosis); 3 people attributed their behavior to the death of a loved one; 3 mentioned financial worries; 1 said pain and disability; and another was concerned with his alcoholism. Thus, any number of precipitating factors and motives may become suicidogenic through a variety of combinations and interactions.[27]

Means of Lethality

Although many older people in Great Britain take overdoses of drugs, other poisons, or gas to kill themselves, the majority employ more active methods, such as cutting, drowning, jumping, hanging, or shooting. This trend is also revealed in the abortive attempts of older people in England, who often employ more violent methods than do the country's youthful attempters.[4]

In the United States, suicides of older people usually leave little doubt that they were intentional. Violent acts, such as shooting, jumping, drowning, and hanging, are typical. Drugs are only used by a minority of geriatric suicides—mostly women—while firearms are unquestionably the major means employed.[9,16,35]

The elderly also have their own special means of committing suicide, including: self-starvation; refusal to follow physicians' orders; not taking medications; engaging in hazardous activities; delaying treatments or operations; and voluntary seclusion.[16,22] Older people also accomplish their suicides "subintentionally" by drinking excessively, by drug abuse, by smoking, and, for those with diabetes, by dietary mismanagement.[55] These gradual processes, which have been labeled "suicidal erosion," are not included in suicide statistics because suicide is viewed conceptually as a single act.[16]

Prevention of Geriatric Suicides

The prevention of suicide in late life may ultimately depend on social measures.[53] The more obvious and immediate of such measures would satisfy the basic economic needs of the aged, would increase occupational security in middle age, and would create a more elastic policy regarding the retirement of older people. In addition, much more serious consideration needs to be given to retirement planning and to examining the needs and interests of the retired elderly.[46]

One researcher suggested surrounding the elderly, particularly males and widowers, with what he called "the protective walls of meaningful social engagement" (part-time or full-time employment, local friendship and neighborhood groups, and additional formal organizations for the aged).[10] He also saw religious and fraternal organizations as having a vital preventative role to perform[11] and wanted to see the elderly themselves used to search for the isolated and potentially suicidal among them.[10] The latter idea could even be carried a step further by soliciting older people to work at suicide prevention centers speaking to older callers.[22]

Since older men seldom turn to suicide prevention centers for assistance, it has been recommended that physicians, clergy, police, nurses, and public welfare workers help to identify the aged with high suicide potential and refer those at risk for appropriate treatment.[129] Senior centers could also be used to identify the potentially suicidal older person.[46]

One research team thought reducing the frequency of depression and providing for its effective treatment would be a major means of ameliorating the problem of geriatric suicide.[16] They also wanted mental health personnel to take the threats of suicide of the aged more seriously and for therapists to schedule extra visits for those who had threatened. Although they emphasized outreach services are imperative to reach depressed people who may have become withdrawn and isolated, they felt *the ultimate answer would be for old age itself to offer the elderly something worthwhile for which to live.*[16]

It is known that in the months immediately preceding their deaths, a very large percentage of older suicidal men are under a physician's care.[2,35,99,124,132] It has also been shown that although older patients will apprise their physicians of their depressed feelings, very few, if any, will voluntarily tell their doctors of their suicidal ideas.[43] The patient's reticence may result mainly from the physician's failure to ask direct questions about the possibility of suicide. Most patients will readily discuss their suicidal feelings when asked.[126] Therefore, at least one path to prevention would lead to increased suicidological education, training, and sensitivity among medical doctors.

Although much of the responsibility for the prevention of geriatric suicides rests with physicians, there is also a great need for more public education.[7] Several suggestions have been offered: (1) psychiatric consultation after hospital care for suicide attempts or for older patients reported as confused, paranoid, or depressed; (2) training of police in suicide intervention; (3) creation of additional suicide prevention agencies; (4) community-sponsored research into suicidogenic factors indigenous to the community; (5) registration of all suicide attempts to facilitate follow-up assistance; (6) greater professional interest in self-destructive behavior in general; and (7) the development of a simple predictive tool for the use of numerous organizations of older people.[7,46]

The following commentary on prevention provides a concise summary:

> We know old people are more likely to suffer mental breakdowns if they are not socially integrated into the community and if they do not feel useful, valued, and loved. We should therefore encourage old people to continue in their occupations for as long as possible—and we must make this administratively possible. Family ties should be kept close: for the lonely, social clubs should be provided, especially in the cities; we should see that retirement and leisure can be happily used; in every way we should foster in the community understanding of the psychologic needs of old people and of the special role they should play as transmitters of the culture's traditions. The older person who feels he is a burden upon his relatives is likely to want to relieve them of that burden by his death.[4]

Intervention in Geriatric Suicides

Perhaps the greatest problem with suicide intervention among the elderly is that few older people know of the crisis intervention services available to them. Even more frustrating to concerned professionals is the tendency of those older suicidal people who do know of the services not to use them or other outpatient community agencies.[46] It has been shown that less than 2 percent of the completed suicides in St. Louis ever contacted the St. Louis Suicide Prevention Center,[121] and virtually identical results were documented in Los Angeles.[134] In 1973 and 1974, out of 8,000 initial calls to the Los Angeles Suicide Prevention Center, only 2.6 percent were from people 60 and older.[17]

A national survey of people 65 and older in England of awareness of the existence and purpose of Britain's major suicide prevention organization, The Samaritans, showed only 41 percent of the 583 people responding had ever heard of The Samaritans, while only 28 percent were familiar with its purpose.[1] Only 10 percent of the respondents knew where the local Samaritan's office was, and 0.5 percent knew the office's telephone number. The random survey also showed older people in the lower socioeconomic classes were less likely to know about The Samaritans. If the lower-class aged commit suicide the most, as has been suggested,[1,50] then those at greatest risk among the elderly in England are the least likely to be familiar with The Samaritans.

The British survey also indicated that a third of the older people questioned in England find it difficult to use the telephone, while 4 percent said they never use one. The isolated elderly in England, who are the most likely to commit suicide, seem more apt to have difficulties using the telephone and therefore are less likely to do so.[1] The implications of this study for older suicides in the United States are difficult to ignore.

At most suicide prevention centers in the United States, efforts to save the desperate older person are blended into the overall program of the agency. Unfortunately, these centers traditionally have not been able to assist some of the groups who need their service the most—the aged, who are unlikely to ask to be saved.[46]

The policy of waiting for clients to telephone or visit the centers means the agencies will not be contacted by the uninformed, socially isolated, and fearful person who has already decided to kill himself. Because today's aged are part of that self-reliant generation that often seems reluctant to utilize even the least threatening of social welfare services, the elderly are unlikely to reach or be saved by the nation's suicide prevention centers.[46] Statistical studies in various areas of the United States have reached the same conclusion. Therefore, the need for outreach efforts to identify, refer, and treat the older suicidal person is apparent.

3

Suicidal Patterns among the Elderly

A deeper understanding of the motivations and patterns most closely associated with geriatric suicides also provides greater insight into the problems faced by many older people who are not suicidal. Thus, an understanding of the suicidal patterns of the elderly is desirable not only for suicide prevention and intervention, but also for its numerous applications to gerontology. However, it is doubtful if this knowledge will do much by itself to lower the geriatric suicide rate since the most prevalent etiological factor appears to be severe physical deterioration.[35] In order to ameliorate the problem, there must first be drastic changes in how our society views and treats its oldest members. Until we are able to effect some of these basic changes, we should expect to see older people continuing to kill themselves in large numbers.

Most suicidal people of all ages appear to have the same basic motivation: the desire to escape from an intolerable situation. During a crisis, the typical potential suicide sees his situation as hopeless and considers himself helpless to alter his predicament.

He begins to believe the only alternative is to escape through death.

As noted previously, the major distinction between geriatric and adolescent suicides is the much more pronounced intent to die in the older population. Unlike young people, the aged rarely attempt suicide.[10,22,34,47] A geriatric suicide attempt is usually a very serious attempt, which only failed because of some peripheral and unanticipated reason (someone coming home unexpectedly and rescuing the attempter). However, suicidal episodes among young people are often characterized by gestures which typically do not cause death. In most cases aged suicidal people truly want to die, while many of their younger counterparts often want to be rescued.

Many older suicidal people do not want to be rescued because they have conditions which cannot be significantly improved. For example, a 16-year-old girl may suddenly become suicidal after her boyfriend announces in a callous manner he does not want to continue dating her. However, once she is aided through her crisis, her suicidal desire will tend to quickly abate, especially after she begins dating someone she likes. Her problem is resolvable.

On the other hand, how do you resolve the problem of an 80-year-old man whose brain has been devastated by cancer? Until we can successfully transplant the brain, there will be no completely satisfactory answer to that question. Even if a cure for cancer were discovered tomorrow morning, how would that triumphant news directly benefit the man whose brain has already been destroyed by cancer? The inescapable conclusion is simply that many older peoples' perceptions of their quandaries as not being resolvable are often rational and valid.

Suicidal Reactions in Late Life

There appear to be eight major patterns of geriatric suicidal behavior. Each pattern is actually a means of reacting to one or more of the "insults of aging." Here is a list of the patterns: (1) the reaction to severe physical illness; (2) the reaction to mental illness; (3) the reaction to the threat of extreme dependency and/or institutionalization; (4) the reaction to the death of a spouse; (5) the reaction to retirement; (6) the reaction to pathological personal relationships; (7) the reaction to alcoholism and drug abuse; and (8) the reaction to multiple factors.

In a general sense, each of these suicidogenic reactions could be subsumed under the last heading, "multiple factors." However, this would negate the most important point of this discussion. Although there is seldom one simple reason why anyone commits suicide, the titles of the first seven reactions represent an attempt to focus attention on the *salient motivation* in any given case of geriatric suicide.

The patterns of geriatric suicides definitely overlap. For example, some people suffering from mental illness may at the same time fear institutionalization; however, others who fear institutionalization may not be mentally ill at all. Therefore, discrete categories are necessary in order to fully understand the various motivations and patterns associated with geriatric suicides.

Also, there may be considerable variation within each pattern. For instance, in "the reaction to the death of a spouse," any two widowers who commit suicide may have remarkably different problems affecting their lives. One widower might be wealthy, while the other might subsist on a fixed and inadequate income. The first widower might have several children, while the second may be childless. One could be a novelist and the other a bus driver. The novelist may have been ill much of his life, while the bus driver may have been the paragon of health. In short, the two men may have little in common other than both being widowers who commit suicide. It is in this sense that no two suicides have precisely the same predisposing factors present in their lives.

As people grow older, they naturally incur more and more significant losses. These losses may cumulatively have a much greater effect than any one of them might have exerted individually. The closer in time the losses occur, and the more unexpected their onset, the greater the inimical effect they seem to have.[35]

This is why several deleterious factors occurring in temporal proximity may become overwhelmingly suicidogenic, particularly in late life when people's defenses and/or resources may already have been totally exhausted.

Whether an older person is able to resolve a suicidal crisis or succumbs to self-inflicted death is very much a function of the ability to cope with stress. Such coping abilities are usually developed in youth, refined through an elaborate trial-and-error process in adolescence, and relied on throughout adulthood. Thus, the person in the midst of a suicidal crisis should certainly be encouraged to utilize a coping strategy that worked well in the past.

The life-versus-death forces in a suicidal crisis may become so precariously balanced that the addition of what appears to be a "minor problem" can seriously imbalance the scale on the side of death.[130] The "minor problem" becomes "the straw that breaks the camel's back"—and provides naive observers with a conveniently simple answer to the enormously complicated question: "Why did he do it?" To think of any one precipitating factor as the sole cause of a suicide is to lose all perspective of the complexity of a suicidal act, not to mention the etiology of the problems that contributed to the act.

Numerous life-versus-death forces and the eight major reactions to suicidogenic stress in the later years are discussed in the following chapters and illustrated by case studies. Much of the information that follows is based on the author's study of 301 cases of suicides committed in Arizona by white males aged 60 and older during 1970 through 1975. Case studies presented are the result of in-depth interviews the author conducted with widows and other survivors of 31 men who killed themselves in Maricopa County, Arizona. Maricopa County includes the populous urban areas of Phoenix, Sun City, Mesa, Tempe, Scottsdale, and Glendale. More than half of Arizona's population resides in Maricopa County. For more detailed data related to the Arizona study, see the following references:[35,37,38,40.]

4

The Reaction to Severe Physical Illness

The most frequently condoned geriatric suicide is the one committed because of severe physical hardship, particularly where extraordinary pain, chronic conditions, and terminal illness are present.[35] During interviews with the author, widows reported they completely understood their husbands' desire for death as a relief from intolerable physical conditions. Some of the women knew, sensed, or assumed their husbands were planning suicide and had no intention of trying to stop them. Because their primary concern was for their husbands' relief, the widows felt suicide had become the only alternative to prolonged agony.

More than 60 percent of the men studied in Maricopa County committed suicide because of extreme illness. About a quarter of the sample had terminal illnesses. Widows of the terminally ill men said they wished there had been some means for their husbands to have legally obtained a drug that would have quickly and painlessly ended the men's misery.* Although they con-

*There is historical precedence for the type of assistance desired by the widows of the men with advanced illnesses. As early as 500 B.C., on the Greek island of Ceos, the state provided poison in a public place to be used by old

doned the suicides, the women deeply regretted their husbands had to resort to self-inflicted gunshots in order to end their pain. That sentiment was especially strong among widows who had discovered their husbands' disfigured bodies.

"Cancer" may very well be the most anxiety-producing word in the English language. Fearing they had cancer, some men in the Maricopa County sample killed themselves to end their dread. Even when several doctors and comprehensive medical tests indicated no malignancy, their anxiety was not ameliorated. One man was so convinced he had the disease, despite his doctors' contradictory opinions, he wrote a suicide note urging his survivors to see the results of his autopsy. Apparently he did not know suicides in Arizona are not given autopsies unless there are equivocal circumstances surrounding the deaths. Because of that policy it will probably never be known if any of the men who feared they had cancer were correct.

When a person takes his life because of an incurable disease, suicide may be considered euthanasia. Under such conditions even people who are usually opposed to suicide will often understand, if not condone, the suicidal act of the terminal patient seeking euthanasia.

In the case histories that follow, one man had suffered six heart attacks, while the other had multiple physical conditions. What these cases share is a clear indication that severe illness can easily become suicidogenic in late life. The ambivalence of the survivors toward the suicidal acts is also illustrated.

---

people who were seriously ill or debilitated. In the first century B.C., according to the Greek geographer Strabo, older people who felt they had lived too long would gather at an annual banquet and drink poison. And in the Greek colony of Masilia, which is now Marseilles, France, a lethal potion was given to those who could justify to certain officials their wish to die.[110]

CASE ONE

Mr. A. was the second of five children. He was described by his widow as a quiet person who continually had "a chip on his shoulder." Someone was always "rubbing him the wrong way," especially his bosses, whom he "just about hated."

For many years Mr. A. had acted "as though the world had done him wrong." When he was in business he would often "kick customers out and tell them to 'go to hell.' " He particularly disliked students or anyone with an education, which was unfortunate because he had lived for many years in a college town. When he was drunk he would become violent and unpredictable.

The son of a domineering father, Mr. A. was one-quarter American Indian. He had few friends, but had been close to one of his brothers; however, his brother's death preceded his own by several years. When his mother died about three years before his suicide, he refused to attend her funeral because he claimed he was sicker than she had been.

Mr. A.'s father-in-law had tried to kill himself in 1924 and 1932. Both attempts were apparently the result of poor business conditions and in both cases he had slashed his wrists. It is not known what influence if any these acts ultimately had on his son-in-law. However, Mr. A. also attempted suicide twice during a five-day period in 1969. The first attempt was with gas and the second involved drugs (although a gun was found near the body that had not been fired). No psychiatric services were obtained for Mr. A. as a result of those incidents. He apparently gave no explanation for his actions, but his widow concluded "he just got tired of taking pills." She said "he had made it clear to me he didn't want a lingering death."

In 1950 Mr. A. experienced the first of six heart attacks. The worst and final one took place in early 1973, only a few months before his suicide. The doctors told his wife he had been dead for half an hour, but they were able to resuscitate him. Mrs. A. was angry and asked the doctors: "Why didn't you just let him go?"

While being operated on for his heart condition, Mr. A. suffered a stroke which left his right hand and the right side of his face paralyzed. The doctors told Mrs. A. the stroke had been caused by "being on the heart-lung machine for too long." The operation was not completely successful and another was performed the following night to close a small artery that was still bleeding.

Mr. A. also developed speech problems. His words would run together and sound like gibberish, and he would cry. After a complete physical examination, it was determined the problem was caused by his medication. His speech problem abated when the medicine was changed.

During the next few months he seemed unhappy and depressed, although he was responding well to physical therapy. Two weeks before his suicide, his physician examined him and reported he was "doing just great." A few days before his death at age 62, a physical therapist was unusually rough with him and he cried from the pain. Mrs. A. felt that event was the catalyst for her husband's suicide even though she believed "he would have done it anyway sooner or later."

The night before his death, Mr. and Mrs. A. had gone out to supper with another couple. They enjoyed themselves and he seemed to his wife to be "at peace with the world and himself . . . somehow relieved." The couple even discussed spending the hot summer months up in the mountains and Mr. A. had agreed to join them. Giving no indication of what he was about to do, he awoke early the next morning and shot himself in the head.

CASE TWO

Mr. B.'s mother died when he was 2 years old. As a result, he was raised by an uncle and was never close to his father. Although he was 64 years old when he took his life, his physical condition had deteriorated to that more commonly associated with a much older man.

Mr. B. had been a salesman and a diabetic most of his adult life. The majority of his physical problems had not become severe until five years before his death. He then began experiencing such a rapid physical decline that even ten operations could not restore his health.

Hemorrhaging caused him to become almost blind and problems with his ears caused him to become virtually deaf. A stroke left one side of his face distorted and made it difficult for him to eat or walk.

A week before he took his life he had undergone another unsuccessful ear operation. The morning before his death he said "Something has popped in my head" and after it burst he screamed to his wife of forty years: "Don't leave me! Don't leave me!" The night before his suicide he said: "They've messed me up again. I'm not going to put up with this."

On the last morning of his life Mr. B. "looked and acted very peacefully." He ate an unusually large breakfast and "seemed contented." After eating, Mr. B. called a taxicab, went to a nearby bank, withdrew some money, and returned home. He later took another taxi, apparently purchased a gun, and returned home "with a brown paper bag."

A neighbor saw Mr. B. walk to the side of his house where he normally never walked. He removed the gun from the bag and shot himself in the head. The neighbor witnessed his suicide and shouted at him to stop, but it is doubtful he heard her or would have complied with her request if he had.

Although his widow was obviously relieved that her husband no longer had to suffer, Mrs. B. was unable to say she would have rather he were out of his misery than still alive and living with her.

5

The Reaction to Mental Illness

A recurrent theme in geriatric suicide literature concerns the close association of mental illness with suicide among the elderly.[4,43] Some researchers have even reported that almost all of the aged suicides they have studied were mentally ill,[4] yet no one seems able to precisely define mental illness.

Consider how often prosecutors and defense attorneys are able to produce "expert witnesses" who come into court after having examined the same person and present diametrically opposed testimony. One group of psychiatrists will attest to the person's sanity while another group, also under oath, will state that the person is insane. Which group is correct?

When trying to discuss suicide in terms of mental illness, it is difficult to distinguish the cause from the effect. Do people kill themselves *because* they are mentally ill or do the stressful forces impinging on their lives *cause* them to become mentally ill immediately before their suicides? In other words, does crisis precipitate the mental illness and cause them to kill themselves or does the mental illness produce the crisis? The answer to this "chicken-or-egg" conundrum seems to depend on which person is being discussed under what circumstances.

It seems reasonable to conclude that a large percentage of geriatric suicides suffer from mental illness at the time of their deaths; however, it would be an exaggeration to say the overwhelming majority of older suicides are mentally ill. In Maricopa County, 23 percent of the suicides had been diagnosed as mentally ill at some time in their lives. It was also determined that 40 percent had relatives who had been diagnosed as mentally ill.

In the two case studies that follow, there was little doubt mental illness was closely involved with the suicidal behavior. In one of the cases, a man set himself on fire, an uncommon means of suicide which, although often fatal, seldom leads to a quick death.

CASE THREE

> Mr. C. had a good marriage and enjoyed good health. Within a period of two years, his mother, oldest brother, brother-in-law, and wife's brother-in-law all died. The losses stunned him; he had a nervous breakdown, and was institutionalized. He received psychiatric treatment and was scheduled for shock treatments, but his family physician obtained his release before he had any. After he recuperated from his breakbown, one of his aunts died. Mr. C. was never again employed.
>
> His widow described him as a man who kept to himself and didn't have many friends. In fact, near the end of his life, he had become so withdrawn that he had essentially stopped conversing with Mrs. C. She had difficulty even getting him to answer yes or no to her questions.
>
> Mr. C. became more despondent following surgery on his prostate and for a hernia. His father had died of

cancer of the prostate and he became convinced he had the same malady. Neither his wife nor his doctors could dissuade him. Even his suicide note indicated his dread: "I can't get well—see autopsy."

He began to have paranoid fantasies and confided in his wife that he thought the sheriff was watching their house and had placed listening devices in some of the rooms. He also complained that "his flesh felt like it was crawling on his bones."

A year before his death, Mr. C. lost faith in all his doctors except for one who had treated him in his native state. His wife suggested he return there for a complete hospital examination. He followed his wife's suggestion, but even the doctor he trusted couldn't find anything wrong with him. He was eventually advised to see a neurologist and did so three days before his death.

Toward the end of his life, Mr. C. often experienced dizziness and complained of pains in his lower chest. Somehow he associated the chest pains with cancer of the prostate and became even more convinced he was following in his father's footsteps. His appetite diminished and he developed sleeping disorders; however, during the last week of his life he began sleeping much better than he had been.

Mr. and Mrs. C. rode bicycles together every morning, but on the day of the suicide his wife could not accompany him because of pains in her legs. He didn't say anything to her when he left, which was not unusual for him. He rode about half a mile to the shell of a home under construction, entered it, and shot himself. The suicide note was found in his shirt pocket. The note notwithstanding, no autopsy was performed because the police did not show the widow her husband's suicide note until after his body had already been cremated.

Mrs. C. was certain the gun her 66-year-old husband used to kill himself had been kept in their house without any bullets. She assumed he must have purchased some bullets shortly before his suicide.

When told of Mr. C.'s suicide, a nurse who worked in his physician's office said: "I expected it." However, she was never asked to explain her remark.

CASE FOUR

Mr. D., the oldest of four children, had worked as a farmer and a carpenter most of his life. He was married to the same woman for 58 years.

In 1972, two years after Mr. D. had suffered a stroke, he began to complain of severe headaches and dizziness. An examination revealed a 1-inch-thick blood clot in his brain and a very serious operation was performed. Although the surgeons were successful in removing the blood clot, they were unable to close a bleeding vein in his brain for fear of permanently paralyzing him. They knew it was only a matter of time until he would form another clot.

After the operation the 78-year-old Mr. D. was angry because he felt "his time to die had come," but his family had caused him to live longer than was necessary by authorizing the operation. He often said "he hadn't enjoyed a minute of life since the operation."

In 1974 Mr. D. experienced a catastrophe. His favorite grandchild, her husband, and their three children were killed when a huge flash flood washed away their camp site. One of the great-grandchildren was never found. Mr. D. never fully recovered from the shock of that tragedy. He would often talk and cry about it until his suicide, almost a year later. During that year one of his close friends died, and his only son died of cancer.

Mr. D. began losing touch with reality. He would

ask who was the woman living in his house. He felt he was living in sin since the woman couldn't be his wife. He would say: "I married the prettiest girl in the school and the woman living with me is someone else who is all wrinkled." Sometimes he imagined two women were living with him—one in the kitchen and one in the bedroom. He would often ask when his wife was coming home.

Three weeks before his death, Mr. D. withdrew all of the money in his checking account. A clerk at the bank alerted the family and they found Mr. D. "wandering in an alley with the check in his pocket."

About two weeks before the suicide, Mr. D.'s physician advised the family to have the 80-year-old man committed to a mental institution because he represented "a danger to himself and to others." The family was in the process of having Mr. D. declared legally incompetent at the time of the suicide. In fact, they were scheduled to go to court only three days after he fatally injured himself.

As far as his son-in-law knew, none of the relatives had told Mr. D. about the pending legal procedures to have him committed. However, the son-in-law could not be certain if Mrs. D. had given her husband any clues.

The evening before the suicide, Mr. D. experienced severe headaches and he paced the floor most of the night. On the final morning of his life, he awoke early and quietly walked to a vacant lot next to his home. On the way he removed a five-gallon gasoline can from a storage bin and after pouring the gasoline on himself, he lit a match. As the flames enveloped him, he moaned and uttered sounds which his daughter, who lived next door, thought "were those of an animal." She looked out the window, saw her father burning, and called for help. Mr. D.'s son-in-law put out the fire.

Mr. D. had suffered third degree burns over 80 percent of his body. His daughter ran to him screaming: "There's been a terrible accident." Mr. D. told her: "This wasn't any accident. I knew what I was doing." He asked: "Am I going to Hell?" His daughter replied: "No, we're taking you to the hospital." He died five days later.

It was his son-in-law's opinion that another large blood clot had caused Mr. D.'s irrational thinking.

6

The Reaction to the Threat of Extreme Dependency and/or Institutionalization

The prospect of becoming extremely dependent and/or institutionalized may represent such a great threat to many older people that it will trigger a suicidal reaction.[35] The institutions may be general or psychiatric hospitals, or more likely, nursing or old age homes. Often what is actually feared is the excessive dependency that is part of almost any institutional setting. Independence appears to be so important to the elderly that many older people would rather die than become debilitated and dependent.[134]

Because the loss of mobility usually leads to increased dependency, it is terrifying to many older people. The loss of a driver's license, the ability to walk, or a limb may result in forced institutionalization or having to live with relatives against one's will. This fear is probably greatest in communities where public transportation is nonexistent or inaccessible to many older people.

Research on the relocation of the aged has clearly indicated a relationship between the loss of cherished and familiar surroundings and increased morbidity and mortality. It would appear that the fear of increased dependency found in so many older persons is justifiable from several perspectives.

In the two case histories presented, the fear of dependency and institutionalization was apparently so acute it had become suicidogenic. One man feared having to return to a nursing home and the other having to reenter a psychiatric hospital.

CASE FIVE

Mr. E. had moved west with a married couple and the three of them purchased and lived in a house together. One day he received a call from a realtor who wanted to show a prospective buyer the house. It was only then he discovered his friends were planning to "sell the house out from under him." He had encountered such treatment many times in his life. His two marriages had ended in divorce, the last one 24 years before his suicide, and both his wives had left him.

Three months after the house was sold, Mr. E. was severely injured in a construction accident when a beam fell on his back. He seemed to recover completely, but a year later he awoke one morning to discover he had suddenly become a paraplegic. Confined to a wheelchair, and retired on a disability pension, he lived in a large house by himself. He did his own cooking and laundry, but depended on neighbors to buy his food.

He began to experience great pain and had to use a catheter because he had lost control of his bladder. After undergoing several operations, he was told by his doctors they could not help him and he would not get better. His dependence on pain-killing drugs grew and he began sleeping much of the time.

Unable to take care of his large house, he eventually

began boarding with another married couple. He found himself quite attracted to the woman; however, the feeling was not mutual. He was elated when the couple developed marital problems and the husband moved out of the house. Imagining himself taking over the former husband's role, he bought the woman gifts, including a ring for her birthday. In the meantime, she met another man, eventually married him, and the new husband moved into the woman's home. Mr. E. was deeply disappointed because he had desperately wanted such an arrangement for himself.

On numerous occasions he threatened to shoot himself if he could not be relieved of his pain. Although he tried to get into various rehabilitation programs, he was consistently rejected because of his age and condition.

He could no longer stand living in the home of the woman he cared for while she was showing so much attention and affection to her new husband. He threatened to leave unless the couple made certain changes in the house and they seized the opportunity to call his bluff by asking when he was leaving.

After having lived in a nursing home for a year and having visited his father in one for several years, he had grown to detest all nursing homes. However, he felt he had no choice but to arrange to live in one once again. About a month before his death at age 63, he took a taxicab to a sporting goods store and bought a gun. The morning he was to enter the nursing home, he shot himself in the head while lying on his bed.

CASE SIX

When they were children, Mr. F. and his sister were often told by their father that they were crazy. In adulthood they both committed suicide.

Mr. F. was a farmer who had loved heavy work and long hours, but became ill with emphysema and had to retire. By then half of his stomach had been removed because of bleeding ulcers. He later developed other ailments which were painful, kept him from driving a car, and prevented him from traveling to see his children. Once a man who had taken enormous pride in being robust and productive, he saw himself rapidly deteriorating.

He did not adjust well to having so much leisure time. After trying several activities, he found he did not enjoy them. Mr. F. didn't have any pets or hobbies and was unable to find anything meaningful to do, so each day he would take long walks through his neighborhood.

He had always been very close to his unmarried sister, but three years before his death she had killed herself by slashing her wrists and ingesting rat poison. Her death had a prolonged, deleterious effect on him.

Mr. F. often told his wife he was no longer of any use to his family and one morning she awoke to discover he had cut his throat with a butcher's knife. He was placed in a mental institution for three weeks and received shock treatments. After his release he continued to see a psychiatrist whenever he was depressed. In fact, he saw the psychiatrist about three days before his suicide at age 63, and was advised to reenter the mental hospital. His reaction was: "I'd rather be dead than be back in the hospital."

The following day he asked his wife if she "could ever do away with him." Mrs. F. reminded him she couldn't even kill a chicken when they lived on their farm.

On the day of his suicide, Mr. F. went to a friend's home and asked to borrow a pistol. He said he thought he had heard a prowler the night before and the friend gave him the gun. Although the friend was not aware of it, Mr. F. had unsuccessfully tried five times to borrow a gun from one of his neighbors. Also, Mr. F.'s son had removed a rifle from their home because "he knew his father wasn't well."

As Mr. F. walked out of the friend's yard, Mrs. F. came riding around the corner on her bicycle. She does not know if he saw her, but she heard a shot, dropped her bicycle, and began running down the street. The friend stopped her and said Mr. F. had shot himself.

For a long time thereafter, Mrs. F. publicly and privately blamed the friend for having given her husband the gun. Apparently the pressure became so great that the friend moved out of the community.

During an interview after her husband's death, Mrs. F. said Mr. F. had not done or said anything to indicate he was about to commit suicide.

7

The Reaction
to the Death of a Spouse

A fifth of the suicides studied in Maricopa County were widowers. Two salient characteristics of the older widowers who killed themselves were found in all the cases studied. The first was that each of the men believed in an afterlife. Faith in an afterlife may have motivated them to join their deceased spouses—a desire that is frequently articulated by older widowed people, both male and female.[33]

The second characteristic was how quickly the men's suicides took place after the death of their wives. In some cases the suicides occurred only a day or two later, which could indicate the men were still in a state of shock at the time of their self-inflicted deaths. Perhaps suicide could have been obviated in those cases if only enough time had passed for the widowers to have become adjusted to their plight. Research supports such speculation.

MacMahon and Pugh have found that the risk of suicide in a widowed population is particularly great during the first year of bereavement.[33] Several other studies, most notably those of Parkes et al. in England, have also demonstrated that the incidence of morbidity and mortality become elevated by as much as

40 percent during the crucial first year following a spouse's death.[128]

The following case histories provide insight into the predicament of the recently bereaved widower. In one of the cases the deceased killed himself the day after his wife's death and in the other a period of only four months had passed since the wife died.

CASE SEVEN

Mr. G. was an extremely strong-willed, disciplined man. Some forty years before his death, he concluded he was an alcoholic, vowed never to drink again, and kept his word. Years later he also stopped smoking in a similar manner. According to his daughter-in-law, "Once he made up his mind about anything or anybody, you could never change it."

Mr. G. hated doctors, hospitals, and taking medication. At various times in his life he had been operated on for gallbladder, prostate, and a slight stroke. Each time he checked himself out of the hospital before doctors would permit him to leave. In his later years he became hard of hearing, developed heart trouble, and had a growth on his vocal cords which limited his speech to soft sounds that often could not be understood.

Whenever his wife became hospitalized, he refused to stay at his children's homes. The only promise he ever asked his children to make was that they would never place his wife in a nursing or old age home.

Mrs. G. was a spiritualist and an artist. She and her husband told people they had spoken with spirits and believed in reincarnation. Mrs. G. had become an invalid during the last year of her life. Mr. G. cooked for her, cleaned their home, and carried her from room to room. He killed himself the day after she died. He was 83 years old at that time and once again he refused to move in with his children. In fact, he was angry they had even suggested the idea.

The day after his wife's death, he was unconsolable and kept moaning: "Why did she have to leave me?" He sat brooding and crying in the dining room of his home, surrounded by many of his relatives. He left the room and his family thought he was getting tissues to wipe his tears. Instead, he went into his bedroom to get his gun and shot himself in the chest.

After the suicide, his daughter remarked: "He felt his purpose in life was over when his wife died."

CASE EIGHT

In prep school and later at the New York Athletic Club, Mr. H. was a swimming star on the same team as Johnny Weismuller.

Shortly after Mr. H. married, his mother moved in with the young couple and stayed for more than twenty years, even though Mrs. H. and her mother-in-law bickered constantly. Mr. H. was highly dependent on his wife for meals, laundry, and other household tasks. They went everywhere together and shared several hobbies. She was even described as "the brains behind his business."

Five years before his death, Mr. H.'s favorite aunt died. Three years later, his best friend and confidant died of cancer. His friend's death shocked him and he never completely adjusted to the loss.

After having been sick for ten years, Mrs. H. be- came seriously ill and died within three months. The loss of his wife was more than Mr. H. could bear. He felt guilty and worried that he could have done more for his wife or had done the wrong things. He felt two of the doctors had not done as much as they could have and refused to pay them.

After his wife's death he became depressed and attempted suicide with some of her medication. The attempt took place about three months before his death. His daughter found him and rushed him to the hospital. He was seen by a psychiatrist, who suggested he temporarily move in with his daughter. However, it is doubtful Mr. H. viewed the suggestion as an alternative because of the negative experience he had after his mother moved into his home.

When he returned home from the hospital, no one in his family discussed his suicide attempt with him.

A few weeks before his death, Mr. H. told his daughter which lawyer to use to settle his affairs "in case anything ever happened to him." He also had a sizable bank account transferred into his daughter's name.

Four months after his wife's death, he shot himself in the head while standing in a swimming pool near his home.

8

The Reaction to Retirement

Today's older generation was imbued with the Protestant work ethic—the positive value placed on working to get what you want and the negative value placed on idleness. Since no merit was seen in recreation, idle hands were considered evil and wasteful, and retirement held no special charm. A man's worth was equated with his productivity; not to be productive was to be a parasite.

At the time these values became ingrained in American consciousness, one could work as long as one's mind and body permitted. Now numerous exogenous factors, such as company policies, union contracts, insurance provisos, plant closings, bankruptcies, and age discrimination may dictate when a worker must retire.

For the person who has not prepared for it, retirement may require one of life's most difficult adjustments. In Maricopa County, a number of survivors described how retirement had harmed the men who committed suicide. The negative effects of not working seemed particularly harmful to men who entered retirement without the hobbies, memberships in organizations, friendship/kin networks, and varied interests that typically occupy the time and attention of many retired men with high morale.[35]

One exasperated retiree who eventually took his life confessed to his daughter that he had chopped down the only tree in their backyard "just so he could have something to do." Other men expressed their disenchantment with retirement by obtaining jobs requiring considerably less skill than they demonstrated in their careers. In one case, a former executive of a major insurance company took a job pumping gasoline.

People approaching retirement should make plans to make late life more enjoyable. Unfortunately, not enough do. Because they assume they will know how to take care of themselves in retirement, many people approach this major transition without benefit of any special preparation. As a result, some find themselves facing unanticipated problems that might have easily been prevented. Of course, others have well-conceived plans that are unexpectedly destroyed.

A positive step toward stemming the tide of geriatric suicides might be a greater emphasis on preretirement and postretirement education, planning, and counseling. Ideally, programs could begin a few years before retirement as part of a gradual withdrawal process. For example, starting four years before retirement, employees could begin four-day work weeks; at three years before retirement, three-day work weeks; and so forth until the employee is fully retired.

Counseling that starts before retirement and continues during the first two years thereafter could monitor the retiree's progress and identify needed assistance. This might be one approach to mitigating "retirement shock" and encouraging more satisfying use of leisure time. Research could then determine if such an arrangement lowers the incidence of suicide among retired workers.

Is it reasonable to expect people who formerly had many professional and social responsibilities to find meaning and fulfillment in their lives after they have been relegated to playing shuffleboard in a retirement community? The profound lack of meaningful social and recreational roles for many older people seriously detracts from the quality of life in the later years. These problems have never been adequately addressed by our society, which may be yet another partial explanation for the number of male suicides in retirement.

Quotations from Suicidal Retirees and Their Survivors

Many survivors had negative comments about the effects of retirement on men in the Maricopa County sample. The following quotations are considered representative of the opinions of families in which retirement became suicidogenic.

"After my father's retirement at 62, it was amazing how quickly he deteriorated mentally and physically."

"My husband started to die the day he was forced to retire at 65, and a little bit more of him died every day after that."

"All that free time weighed so heavily on him. It was just like a weight hanging around his neck."

"Retirement hurt my husband in more ways than I could tell you."

Perhaps the most revealing commentary is provided by the statements of three retirees shortly before their suicides.

"Ever since I stopped working I've felt like I was in the way all the time."

"I regret giving up work more than any other decision I ever made. Now that I'm retired I'm not worth anything. I'm just a vegetable."

"Retirement is the worst word in the English language. I'm sorry I ever heard of it."

9

The Reaction to Alcoholism and Drug Abuse

The prolonged use of alcohol was clearly related to the suicidal behavior of a number of the older men in the Maricopa County sample. About 20 percent of the suicides studied were described by their survivors as "alcoholic," while another 6 percent were said to have been "heavy or problem drinkers." It was not possible to determine if a given alcoholic was so drunk at the time of his suicide that he was unaware he was about to kill himself. However, heavy drinking over a protracted period is in itself such self-destructive behavior that it has long been viewed as a "slow form of suicide."[122]

It was quite common for the widow of an alcoholic suicide to report that when her husband was sober he had been "one of the nicest, kindest people you would ever want to meet." Another phenomenon noted was that the suicidal threats of alcoholics or men with "alcoholic tendencies" were usually taken less seriously by their families than the threats of nondrinkers.[35]

When we consider the relationship between suicide and alcohol, another "chicken-or-egg" type of question comes to mind. Do people commit suicide because alcohol releases pent-up suicidal impulses, or do people drink to become "brave" enough to kill themselves? Both statements are probably true to some degree in the majority of alcohol-related suicides.

The alcoholics in Maricopa County who killed themselves had apparently been drinking to excess for many years—in several cases for more than twenty years. Two-thirds of the alcoholic suicides were also addicted to drugs. It was also found that 35 percent of all the older suicides studied—whether alcoholic or not—were addicted to or heavily dependent on drugs. The most commonly abused drugs were analgesics, barbiturates, and soporifics. Valium was frequently mentioned by survivors and one man was said to have "eaten aspirin like candy."

Most geriatric drug abusers began using drugs innocently. For instance, a man experiencing insomnia would begin to use a soporific to help him to become sleepy. He would gradually increase the dosage and might combine the drug with alcohol. Finally, the man would feel he could not sleep without several sleeping pills and/or large amounts of alcohol. Thus, the reliance on drugs often went hand-in-hand with a dependence on alcohol. The result was usually a strong addiction to either or both.

Alcohol plays a crucial role in the two case histories that follow. In one, the deceased had lived an unstable life for many years and had become quite dependent on tranquilizers. Two suicide attempts had preceded his death. In the other case, the suicide took place unexpectedly and without warning.

CASE NINE

> After he became an alcoholic, Mr. I.'s first wife divorced him. Later he remarried and stopped drinking for fifteen years. For no apparent reason—even Mr. I. said he did not understand why—he suddenly began drinking again. His second wife, six years his senior,

said that when he was not drinking he was an amiable and hard-working man.

For many years Mr. I. had been a spray painter in a factory. The color of the paint he used last could be seen when he coughed into a handkerchief. Eventually he developed tuberculosis and was in a sanatorium for a year and a half, although several times he became angry and left without medical approval. The top lobe of his right lung was removed and for the rest of his life he experienced difficulty breathing. He had stomach problems for many years, which had been diagnosed as ulcers; however, he suspected he had cancer of the stomach.

His employment history was checkered. Whenever he would get angry on the job, he would quit.

Information about two previous suicide attempts was sketchy, but it appeared he swallowed arsenic about thirty years before his death and was saved by stomach pumping. About three years before his death, he swallowed fifteen Valiums and again had his stomach pumped. Throughout his adult life he often threatened suicide.

Mr. I.'s mother died in a mental hospital. She had been institutionalized six times. Two of her brothers had also been in mental institutions and another of Mr. I.'s uncles had killed himself.

Because of his chronic alcoholism, Mr. I. was seeing a psychiatrist at the time of his suicide. Mr. I. had previously been institutionalized for a week after he tried to shoot his wife. When he was drunk, he would often beat her. Once he threatened her by saying: "I could go in there any night and choke you to death and there wouldn't be a thing you could do to stop me." On another occasion, he told her: "If I can't live with you, no one will." She finally grew tired of his abuse, separated from him, and was suing for divorce at the time of his death.

When drunk he was not responsible for his actions. Twice he sold his automobiles to obtain money to buy alcohol; he sold one for $25. Besides smoking more than two packs of cigarettes a day for many years, he had become reliant on Valium. Because of his chronic alcoholism, he was receiving social security disability benefits.

A month before his death he wrote a "To Whom It May Concern" letter and placed it in a tin box where he kept important papers. The letter contained instructions stating he did not want any funeral service, flowers, or obituary. He also said he wanted to be buried in a sports shirt and slacks, not a suit.

On the morning of his suicide, he came to his wife's home. He had obviously been drinking and had brought a half-filled bottle of liquor with him. He asked to see their dog and after petting it, went out on the steps in front of the house and laid down. He pulled out a gun and showed it to his wife. She struggled to get it away from him, but he still managed to shoot himself in the head. Because her hand was on the pistol when it fired, she received powder burns.

The last thing the 60-year-old Mr. I. did before shooting himself was take a drink.

CASE TEN

Mr. J. had been an alcoholic for many years. However, he had been able to hide his drinking problem by not missing any time from work and by locking himself in his bedroom when he drank. His pattern was not to drink for a few days and then to go on a binge.

His marriage appears to have been an unusually good one until his wife underwent a hysterectomy. After the operation, she refused to return to work and began drinking quite heavily, which she continued to do until she died twelve years later.

It is not clear exactly when Mr. J. began drinking heavily, but it is known that he had experienced prolonged sexual frustration after his wife's hysterectomy. He very much wanted to have children, but his wife was adamantly opposed to having a family.

When his wife died, Mr. J. married, after a brief courtship, a widow whose husband and son he had known for many years. He seemed to have become regenerated in his new marriage. He was happy to have home-cooked meals again and began enjoying a sexual life. Most of all, he seemed thrilled to finally have a family of children and grandchildren.

At the time of the second marriage, the economy had been sagging and business was poor. Although he was financially comfortable enough not to have to work, Mr. J. began to worry about business and became depressed. His employer held a large sales contest, with a trip to Hawaii as the first prize. Mr. J. fantasized about honeymooning in Hawaii and fully expected to win the contest. However, he placed second, didn't win anything, and was deeply disappointed. The contest ended only a few months before he ended his life.

About two weeks before his suicide, he began drinking even more than usual. That was around the anniversary date of his first wife's death, although his second wife said no particular mention was made of the anniversary.

On the final day of his life, the 65-year-old Mr. J. visited "his new family," but insisted he and his wife return home early so he could watch a gangster movie on television. He began drinking as soon as they arrived home and continued to drink throughout the evening. After the movie he went to sleep in the bedroom where he usually slept when he was drunk.

Later he awoke in the middle of the night and turned on some lights. His wife said to him: "Why don't you get under the covers? You must be cold." He replied, "Never you mind," and returned to his bedroom. Shortly thereafter he shot himself in the forehead. His wife, who was deaf in one ear, had rolled over on her good ear and never heard the shot. Realizing the lights were still on, she got up a few minutes later to check on her husband and found him dead. He did not leave a will or a suicide note.

10

The Reaction to Pathological Personal Relationships

Many older people have consistent patterns of pathological personal relationships, and because of this, they invariably suffer many disappointments. In a psychological and social sense, they are slowly "nickeled and dimed to death" by their continual disappointment. Therefore, their reactions to the relationships result in "suicidal erosion."

Some older people with pathological personal relationships may have had poor marriages but never separated or divorced. Others may have tried to exert a tyrannical control over their children and have been unable to relinquish that control even after their children matured. Threatened by their children's ability to function on their own, this type of dictatorial parent may even attempt to dominate their children's families.

When these parents finally realize they can no longer control their families, their self-images suffer. When their lowered self-esteem is combined with other personal losses more typically associated with the aging process, the effect may be suicidogenic. Such a progression was especially noticeable in cases where the domineering parent with a tarnished self-image either would not accept, or did not directly benefit from, professional intervention.[35]

The more they attempt to dominate, the further away they tend to push those who are important to them. The further away they push the significant people in their lives, the more their control of those people is diminished. This vicious cycle may repeat itself for years until the disappointed person finally attempts to resign himself to what he perceives as "defeat," but discovers he cannot tolerate his depreciated self-image. Unable to control as desired and unable to adjust to the resultant ego damage, he may then perceive no alternative to suicide.

Not all people displaying this syndrome have pathological relationships with their children. Some have pathological relationships with their spouses, siblings, other relatives, and friends. But in each case it is extreme disappointment in those relationships that appears to point these people toward suicide.[35]

The two case histories that follow describe this reaction, one in a family with three children and another without children. Note the disappointment these people experience in their relationships with others and themselves.

CASE ELEVEN

Several times in Mr. K.'s life he had completely stopped smoking, drinking, and using drugs; however, he had always resumed those habits. The last time he stopped was about a month before his death and he had made a point of telling his wife how good he felt. He had begun those activities again and was strongly reliant on five medications and was drinking heavily at the time of his suicide.

Mr. K. had been drinking heavily since he was 19 years old. He had experienced stomach problems, a hiatus hernia, a gallbladder operation, and was suspected of having ulcers. He would often say, "Well, I might as well end it all," whenever he would get frustrated.

Mr. K.'s father died of emphysema four years before his suicide and he had been terribly distressed by watching his father die. During his last years, his father wheezed almost constantly, and Mr. K. had developed a serious wheezing problem. He feared he was developing emphysema. A few weeks before his death, he saw a doctor about his wheezing and was given a cough medicine.

Extremely successful in business, Mr. K. had amassed a fortune in land and cattle. His life seemed to revolve around his three children and he showered them with lavish gifts of land, cars, and trips to Europe. However, each child became a source of unhappiness and disappointment to him.

His oldest child was married with two children when she began having an affair and became pregnant by her paramour. She abandoned her husband and children and began drinking heavily. She divorced her husband and married her lover, but her second husband became embroiled in various legal battles with Mr. K. He did not like either of his oldest daughter's husbands. Because of the negative feelings associated with the litigation, his daughter told him she never wanted to see him again, nor did she want him to ever see her children. He was deeply hurt by her statement.

The middle child abandoned his wife and four children to begin living with a woman his mother described as a "barmaid." The son was unemployed, drinking heavily, divorcing his wife, and estranged from his girlfriend when his father committed suicide. Mr. K. did not like the son's wife, girlfriend, or in-laws.

The youngest daughter had married a homosexual. When Mr. K. discovered his son-in-law was gay, he attacked the man with a gun and threw him out of his house. The daughter had a child with her husband, but eventually divorced him and remarried. Mr. K. did not like either of her husbands. Between her marriages he took his youngest daughter to a psychiatrist, who told him that he was the cause of many of his daughter's problems. Upon hearing that, Mr. K. threatened to "smash a chair over the psychiatrist's head" and stormed out of the office.

The night before his suicide he drank a fifth of bourbon and almost drowned when he drove his pickup truck into an irrigation ditch. He nearly cried while describing this incident to his wife.

The next morning the son's mother-in-law called to say she could no longer manage all four of the grandchildren who had been left in her care. She planned to bring two of the children to stay at Mr. K.'s house, and arrived shortly after she had called. When she left, Mr. K. went into his bedroom and shot himself. He was 61 years old. Mrs. K. said he had told her he did not feel he could take care of young children anymore. She felt he was angered by the arrival of his two grandchildren and their other grandmother, whom he detested.

CASE TWELVE

Mr. L. had a very unhappy and unfortunate childhood. His mother was dull-witted and his father was brutal, domineering, and vicious. What appears to have been a major turning point in Mr. L.'s emotional development occurred when his drunken father beat the child's dog to death in front of him when he was 8 years old. Mr. L. continued to recall that event and cry about it sixty years later.

A deeply troubled man, he had talked about suicide for 30 years, although he had not made any previous attempts. Mr. L.'s younger sister once attempted suicide by drinking gasoline and one of his neighbors had committed suicide.

The distinguishing characteristic of Mr. L.'s life was his self-pity. He was sad most of the time, and attributed his hapless existence to being "born under an unlucky sign." He was addicted to violent shows and when he saw people die on television, he would ask why he was not allowed to join them. All of his life he had avoided professional help, saying: "They'd just say I was crazy and put me away."

When Mrs. L. met him, he was working in the garage where she parked her car. She found him sitting on the curb crying and threatening to kill himself, so she talked him out of it by convincing him to marry her instead. They were married three months later.

Mr. L. did not smoke, drink, or gamble, but he had numerous affairs during his marriage. One woman he had been seeing became pregnant and claimed Mr. L. was the father of her child, although it was common knowledge she had been having relations with several men. Over a period of years he paid the woman $5,000 toward the child's support. The child was institutionalized because of severe retardation. Mr. L. brooded over this situation for about 15 years until his death at 69. His wife did not want children because she was afraid her mother-in-law's feebleminded condition was inheritable.

Although he was an unusually healthy man and particularly competent in his work, he had been forced by his employer to retire at 65. His retirement signaled the beginning of a rapid mental and physical decline.

The only friend he ever had died about six months before Mr. L.'s suicide. A few days later Mr. L.'s brother-in-law died. Afterward Mr. L. was unusually moody. Mrs. L. said: "Most of the time he would just sit in his shell."

His wife claimed that Mr. L.'s brother had talked

him into trying to obtain ownership of her automobile by burning the title and using falsified documents to obtain a new one. She alleged Mr. L.'s brother wanted him to have her declared legally incompetent so both men could control her possessions. She also accused her husband of trying to kill her three times; however, her accusations could not be confirmed and may have been confabulations.

Several members of Mr. L.'s family were anxious to inherit from him or his wife and wrote to him describing the objects they wanted after his or her death. He was disgusted by their avarice and burned their mail.

When his wife was told she only had a year to live, Mr. L. came to the hospital crying and saying he did not know what he would do if she died. However, she came home shortly afterwards and outlived him by several years.

On the final morning of his life, Mr. L. had received something in the mail that upset him so much he burned it. He told his wife, "If anybody tries to come in here and take any of your possessions, I'll blow their damned heads off." He brooded most of the afternoon and then went into the back yard and shot himself in the stomach. Even though he owned a shotgun, he used his wife's shotgun to kill himself.

His suicide note to Mrs. L. said: "I know you've hated me. Now you can live with your hate." His wife did not go into the back yard for several hours after she heard the gunshot because she was "afraid her husband would shoot her, too." Soon after the news of Mr. L.'s death reached his family, his relatives began calling the widow to demand their shares of his estate.

11

The Reaction
to Multiple Factors

There are probably as many reasons why people kill themselves as there are people who die from self-inflicted deaths. Perhaps the only observation that can be made with assurance is that there is invariably more than one reason for a suicide. For instance, no one kills himself because he has a terminal illness. He kills himself because of the pain it would cause him, the emotional drain his family would bear, the financial problems that might result, the desire to be remembered as a robust person, the wish to control when death will occur, and any number of other reasons.

If there seems to be a single cause for a geriatric suicide, the death may be thought of in terms of one of the seven reactions discussed in the previous chapters. If several causes seem almost equally responsible for the suicide, the act may be considered a reaction to multiple factors. Although a case could be argued for subsuming all seven of the other reactions under the "multiple factors" heading, doing so would seriously detract from an understanding of those cases in which one motivation is predominant.

Case Thirteen illustrates how numerous inimical factors can synergistically have a lethal effect on an older person's perception of the quality of life. Note how no one factor was overwhelmingly suicidogenic; yet the result of one problem being piled on top of another was the pulling of the trigger that finally relieved the man of his burdens.

In a simplistic sense, it could be said the man in Case Thirteen died because he lost his "will to live." But to say that and nothing further would indicate a lack of understanding of the "multiple factors" category. People do not awake in the morning, yawn, stretch, and then spontaneously lose their "will to live." Such a crucial loss is the result of a lengthy and complex process of erosion. In the cases that follow, that erosion is seen as the combined effect of multiple factors.

CASE THIRTEEN

Mr. M.'s mother died before he was 5 years old and he was raised by his father, who was said to have been a tyrant. His father once "loaned" him to a neighboring farmer in exchange for a pig. The boy's work paid for the pig.

Mr. M. married and had two children, but his wife died of tuberculosis while the children were quite young. He later remarried and had two more children. He did not confide in his children, but had an extremely close and affectionate relationship with his second wife.

He was a devout Catholic who went to mass every Sunday at 6:00 A.M., including the Sunday on which he shot himself to death. A railroad employee most of his life, he began working as a carpenter when the railroad transferred his department to another state.

Mr. M. always avoided medical examinations. In fact, his appendix once burst while he was home because he had refused to see a doctor for his pain. He never served in the military because he was deaf in one ear and had ulcers.

Thirty years before his death, Mr. M. had a friend whose wife killed herself. Within a year the friend had also killed himself. Mr. M. was terribly upset and continued to speak of it years later.

At different times he owned three homes, but whenever he had to decide to buy or sell one of them he had always became upset. While visiting his brother in the Pacific Northwest, he became interested in buying a summer house located only a block from his brother's home. When he returned from his trip he agonized over whether or not to buy the home. The decision weighed on his mind and completely overwhelmed him. In order to put his mind at ease, his children urged him to buy the home and stressed how advantageous "a summer place" would be. His children now fear he interpreted their encouragement as "we don't need you near us, Dad." Although he eventually bought the house, he worried if he had made the right decision. Ironically, he never lived in the house.

Another problem weighing on his mind was his son, who was angry with him and berated him in a series of letters about the mistreatment he felt he had suffered from his father as a child and adolescent. Apparently, much of what his son had alleged was true. The son planned to bring his wife and four children to visit his father for Christmas; however, Mr. M. killed himself in late October.

A year before his suicide, Mr. M.'s 8-year-old niece died of a heart condition. She had been sick since birth and was not protected by medical insurance. Mr. M. was deeply moved by the child's death and gave her parents $100 toward the medical bills. Only a week before his suicide, the 19-year-old son of a close friend was killed in an automobile accident. Mr. M. was also shaken by that event.

Although he had formerly been a very active man, during the last four months of his life he almost never left home. He hated seeing his wife always sitting at home with him and once remarked to her: "I'm holding you back."

While working around the house, Mr. M. would suddenly begin to cry. When his family asked him what was wrong, he would tell them, "I am very sick." He continued worrying about the summer house, his son's impending visit, and feared that the social security system was going bankrupt.

His daughter said: "He had lost all of his gaiety and lightheartedness. We knew something was wrong with him those last few weeks." Mr. M.'s sister felt he might be suicidal, but didn't tell anyone until after his death.

Mr. M. lost his appetite, began losing weight, and developed insomnia. Although he was a man who would have to be "half dead before he would go to a doctor's office," he began visiting doctors voluntarily. The doctors found nothing physically wrong with him, although he continued to plead, "I'm very sick."

Only two weeks before his death, while in a doctor's office, he began crying for no apparent reason. When the doctor asked him what was wrong, he replied, "I don't know." The doctor gave him several sleeping pills, a prescription for more, and told him to return in two weeks. Mr. M. apparently did not understand he could have used the prescription to obtain more sleeping pills, so he rationed the ones he had over a two-week period and only slept about every third night.

His daughter became increasingly concerned about her father's condition and spoke with her doctor. The doctor listened to her story and said he felt Mr. M. should seek psychiatric help, but he first wanted Mr. M. to see an internist to be certain there wasn't anything physically wrong. Mr. M. was scheduled to see the internist the following Monday, but killed himself the day before his scheduled appointment, at age 63.

Two days before his death, Mr. M. and his family heard someone wanted to buy a rifle like Mr. M. owned. His wife suggested he sell the rifle since he never used it. He agreed and called the man who wanted to buy it. The man was eager to look at the rifle, but said that if he were unable to see it that night, he would definitely be there the following Monday night. To prepare for his visit, Mr. M. brought out the rifle, but the man didn't come. On Sunday Mr. M. used the rifle to kill himself. The following night the man called to say he was coming over the buy the rifle.

CASE FOURTEEN

The product of a cruel father and a very unhappy childhood in Austria, Mr. N. was already an alcoholic when he was 29 years old. After he beat his wife and she divorced him, he joined Alcoholics Anonymous. He had been sober for five years when he remarried the same woman. She described their life together as "so miserable it was like being in a concentration camp." They rarely, if ever, had intimate relations during either of their marriages.

Mr. N. was a precise person who lived his entire life "by the minute and the second." Because he was obsessed with money, he refused to pay for any of his wife's bills. She said "she took that for granted when she married him." He once told his wife that when he walked through the supermarket and saw how high the prices were he would "shiver and tremble all over."

Mr. N. had been raised in a "suicidal family."

While still living in Austria (a country with one of the highest suicide rates in the world), his grandfather, an uncle, an aunt, and his father had killed themselves. Mr. N.'s mother had seriously attempted suicide by trying to jump to her death. Mr. N. spoke of his own suicide for many years. He told his stepdaughter, "My entire family killed themselves, so I must kill myself too." He told his wife he was afraid to have any children "because of all the suicide in his family."

He had no friends, rarely smiled or laughed, and often wondered why he was born. He scoffed at humor on television, saying, "Life is not humorous and anyone who laughs about it is an idiot."

Mr. N. never went to doctors because he didn't want to pay their fees. Five years before his suicide, he saw a therapist at a mental health clinic, who said that Mr. N. was obsessed with money. Mr. N. never returned because he said the $3 fee charged for the hour sessions was too expensive.

Four years before his death, Mr. N. lost $45,000 by investing in an apartment house. He was a serious gambler who studied horse racing "as though he were doing deep research." During the stock market decline in 1974, he lost $20,000 in various investments.

Shortly after his sister became widowed, Mrs. N. suggested they invite the woman to move into their home. He agreed, but they both regretted their decision because he argued with his sister much of the time she lived with them.

Mr. N. was a very healthy man, but his wife was diagnosed as having cancer of the pancreas and pronounced terminal. He was deeply troubled by the possibility his wife would die and leave him with the sister he hated.

In his last year, at the age of 67, Mr. N. had begun to work part time in a liquor store. He argued with many of the customers and was afraid of losing his job. He worried that he would not be able to find another job at his age, even though there was no financial need for him to work. Yet he was terrified of going to work because the same man had robbed the store three times. Because the robber threatened Mr. N. with a gun, the manager purchased a pistol to be kept in the store for protection. That was the gun Mr. N. used to kill himself.

A few days before he killed himself he asked his stepdaughter if she had any sleeping pills. He told her he needed them because, "I want to get out."

Nothing unusual happened the day of his suicide except he left his lunch at home. At lunchtime he shot himself in the head. His widow felt he was too methodical a man to have forgotten his lunch.

12

The Role of the Physician in Geriatric Suicides

Many physicians are unaware of the seriousness and scope of the geriatric suicide problem in the United States or of how they could assist in its amelioration.[108] Several studies have shown that approximately 75 percent of all people who kill themselves consult a physician shortly before their fatal acts.[2,22,116,124,140]

Suicide attempters also visit physicians shortly before their suicidal episodes. Researchers in Melbourne, Australia, reported 74 percent of a group of attempters had recently been treated by a physician.[96] In the United States, another research team found 60 percent of their subjects had been under medical care at the time of their attempts.[124]

Other investigators in the United States have suggested that perhaps 10 percent of all suicides see a physician on the day of, or immediately before, their self-inflicted deaths.[132] It therefore seems reasonable to conclude, as most suicidologists have, "suicidal people seek out physicians as potential rescuers."[118] Thus, physicians are clearly in an ideal position to recognize and respond to potentially suicidal patients.

The suicidal elderly display a distinct pattern of medical contact. In Arizona, it was found that more than 77 percent of the geriatric suicides studied had seen a physician within a month of their deaths and 29 percent had seen a physician within a week before the suicides.[35] (See Table 1.) A study in England showed that the corresponding figures were 70 percent and 47 percent, respectively.[2] In Ireland, 55 percent of the older suicides studied had recently been to a doctor and about a quarter had seen a psychiatrist.[57]

If so many people contemplating suicide visit their doctors shortly before killing themselves, why don't physicians detect the suicidal motivations of their patients? Two doctors have suggested an explanation: (1) Suicide is a taboo subject that most people don't want to discuss; (2) Suicides arouses considerable anxiety in physicians; (3) Medical personnel rarely receive adequate training in the recognition and management of the suicidal patient; (4) Physicians usually don't have the sociopsychological knowledge needed to be sensitive to the familial aspects of suicide.[131]

There is no doubt that suicide is a taboo subject.[107] Several studies have indicated a particularly high suicide rate among physicians.[95] Therefore, it seems quite likely a face-to-face encounter with a suicidal patient would be a stressful event even for the most competent of doctors. Perhaps this anxiety factor tends to dull physicians' sensitivity to the suicidal clues their patients so often present.

Lack of formal training in suicidology also decreases a physician's chances of recognizing the imminence of suicide in a patient. Nowhere in their extensive educations do physicians normally receive training in suicide prevention, intervention, or postvention. These are subjects that have basically been overlooked by medical schools and continuing education programs for physicians.

Even if a physician suspects his older patient is suicidal, referring him to a psychiatrist may not solve the problem because many psychiatrists will not knowingly accept a suicidal or older patient for treatment.[117] Some practitioners shy away from such patients because they have low status; they seem to consider them not worth the time involved.[21,114] Of course, being under psychiatric care certainly doesn't preclude the possibility of suicide.[113] About a quarter of older Irish people studied killed themselves after receiving psychiatric care.[57]

The physician may also face the frustrations associated with treating an older patient and/or deciding how much medication to prescribe to a suspected suicidal person. The psychiatrist's fears that the patient may use the medication as the means of suicide may indeed be justified, particularly with women.

Because of societal proscriptions against the admission of any sign of weakness, older suicidal men often feel constrained from seeking or accepting psychiatric assistance. Instead, they are likely to visit a physician and complain of physical discomfort or depression.[35] It has also been shown that although older patients will discuss depressed feelings with their doctors, very few will voluntarily talk about their suicidal thoughts. The patient's reticence may result from the physician's not asking direct questions about the possibility of suicide.[43] Many patients will readily discuss their suicidal feelings when questioned.[126] But if the physician does not probe deeper than the patient's superficial complaints, he may not see the suicidal scenario unfolding before him.

The following case study provides a vivid example of the inability of a family physician and a psychiatrist to successfully detect the suicidal clues presented by an older patient.

Table 1

Final Visits to Physicians by White Male Suicides 60 and Older in Maricopa County, Arizona, during January 1, 1971 through June 30, 1975

When Men Were Last Seen by a Physician	Number of Men	Percentages	Cumulative Percentages
Same day as the suicide	1	3.23	3.23
One week or less before suicide	9	29.03	32.26
One month or less before the suicide	13	45.16	77.42
One year or less before the suicide	3	9.68	86.66
More than a year before the suicide	4	12.93	99.99
TOTAL	31		

CASE FIFTEEN

Mr. O. was the seventh of eight children. His parents died within six months of each other when he was 14 years old. All his siblings had obtained an education except him and he was to regret he hadn't for the remainder of his life. He felt frustrated because he had never risen above a clerical position although he had worked for the same company for many years. The company "suggested" he retire at 60 and he followed the suggestion.

Two years before his death, Mr. O. was traumatized to learn his wife had cancer and required a radical mastectomy. His secretary said he was a "complete wreck" during that period. When talking to his son about the cancer he cried, something he did only rarely.

A year before Mr. O.'s suicide, one of his friends shot himself to death. He anguished over the man's suicide and kept asking his wife why anyone would take his own life. He told her, "You'd have to be out of your mind to do something like that."

Because of his sinus problems, Mr. and Mrs. O. sold their comfortable brick house in Ohio and bought a mobile home in Arizona. Many problems developed with the mobile home and Mr. O. became increasingly unhappy he had purchased it. He told his wife, "How could I have done this to you . . . to bring you out here . . . to have sold such a lovely home for this?" He acted as though he had brought her to Arizona against her will, which was certainly not true.

Mr. and Mrs. O. arrived in Arizona shortly before the hottest time of the year and both of them found the heat oppressive. Soon after they arrived, Mr. O. began to repeat an expression he had never used before: "It's too baffling." Although he had always been the decision-maker in the family, he became unable to make decisions.

He became convinced he couldn't sell his mobile home without losing a great deal of money, yet he yearned to return to his home town in Ohio, where his closest friends lived. Because he was becoming increasingly depressed, Mrs. O. wrote to two of his friends and asked them to visit her husband. They did so, but only for one night on their way to the West Coast. The friends urged Mr. O. to return to his home town even if it were only for a few months. He said he wanted to go back, but he couldn't afford to pay rent there and also have a home in Arizona. They told him he could stay in their large home. When they left, he seemed even more depressed and told his wife he was sorry he wasn't going with them.

To deal with his acute depression, his wife took him to see their family doctor. The physician suggested they go back to Ohio for a few months as a "trial visit," but Mr. O.'s response was only: "It's too baffling." He told the doctor that he couldn't afford to pay rent in Ohio and have a home in Arizona and that he couldn't sell his mobile home without losing much of his investment. The doctor prescribed an antidepressant drug.

Several symptoms revealed Mr. O.'s extreme anxiety and depression. Among them were insomnia, anorexia, impotence, lethargy, and profuse perspiring. Mr. O. continued to agonize over having sold his home, having brought his wife to "this awful place," and having retired. He spoke about how useless he had felt since retiring.

Mrs. O. took her husband to a psychiatrist, who saw him only once and concluded there was nothing wrong with him. Next his wife took him to see their son in California. The son arranged for Mr. O. to see a psychologist, which he did on five occasions. The psychologist thought Mr. O. was harboring a deep-seated anger toward Mrs. O., which upset Mr. O. even more than he had been. After his sessions with the psychologist, he would plead with his wife, "But I'm not angry with you; I'm not." The psychologist suggested he not return to Arizona but go directly to Ohio for an extended visit. Mr. O. didn't take the advice and kept repeating, "It's too baffling." A month later he killed himself.

The night before his suicide, he and his wife visited some friends. He seemed "quite relieved" and was joking and laughing so much his wife thought his antidepressant medication had finally begun to work.

On the last day of his life he ate a small breakfast, kissed his wife on the cheek, and started to leave for his part-time job. Mrs. O. said to him, "Let's just think positively today." He looked very sad, but said, "I'll try."

At his office, he wrote all morning. His secretary said he had thrown away many sheets of paper, but kept writing. Then he left work early, saying he had something important to do, and drove to the bank of a canal about a mile and a half from his home. He carefully laid out his keys, wallet, and suicide note on the seat of the car, sat on the bank of the canal, and shot himself in the head. He was 61 years old.

In his suicide note Mr. O. claimed, "I'm getting worse and I don't think I can be cured." He ended the note with a prayer.

His wife thought he had shot himself at the canal rather than at home so she wouldn't be the person to find him. She said he had liked to swim in a canal as a child.

After Mr. O.'s suicide, his physician wrote to Mrs. O. saying how sorry he was for not having detected the depth of Mr. O.'s depression. The doctor said if he had realized the gravity of the situation he would have placed Mr. O. in an institution.

Even with the assistance of a family physician, a psychiatrist, and a psychologist, Mr. O. still managed to become a suicide statistic. It appears none of the professionals he saw questioned him about his suicidal feelings. Mr. O.'s family recognized his "cry for help" and sought professional assistance, but the help he received never focused on the possibility he might kill himself. No one dealt with the most basic issue in question: "Would this man kill himself before he could be treated?"

13

The Cooperation of
Some Wives
in Their Husbands' Suicides

Many geriatric suicides could not be accomplished without the assistance of a cooperative spouse. Some of these suicides involve euthanasia, others result from the wife's subconscious desire for or ambivalence toward her husband's death, while most are facilitated by the wife's apparent inability to take any determined and appropriate action during a crisis. The cooperation may be overt or covert, but the irreversibility of the result is the same: the successful suicide of the husband.

Three patterns of spouse-assisted suicides were observed in Maricopa County. The first involved men whose illnesses were so extreme that their suicides could more accurately be seen as euthanasia. Although the wives of these men had considerable advance notice of their husbands' impending suicides, they didn't try to intervene because of their tacit approval of suicide as a means of ending devastating illness. Case Sixteen illustrates this type of cooperation.

Chapter 13 originally appeared under the title "Cooperation of Some Wives in Their Husbands' Suicides" in *Psychological Reports* 44:39–42 (February 1979) and is reprinted with permission.

CASE SIXTEEN

When Mr. P. was 25 years old, married, with a young child and his wife pregnant again, he was told he had muscular dystrophy. He eventually developed other painful conditions, such as ulcers, hemorrhoids, and arthritis of the spine.

A very active man when he was younger, Mr. P. had become overwhelmed by his illnesses and confined to a wheelchair for the last ten years of his life. He referred to the wheelchair as "his coffin on wheels."

Mr. P. apparently had a good marriage until three years before his death, when he became increasingly paranoid. He accused his wife of seeing other men, who existed only in his imagination, and became abusive when she would deny his accusations. He would check on her whereabouts while she was working.

Realizing he was venting much of his frustration on his wife, he grew deeply depressed and voluntarily sought a psychiatrist's assistance. The doctor attested to Mr. P.'s paranoid condition. He became remorseful about his abuse of his wife and told her shortly before his suicide, "I can't keep doing this to you."

Mrs. P. worked only blocks from their home. Every morning when she left for work, her husband sat by the window and waved goodbye to her. That was his daily morning ritual, but never at lunchtime, even though his wife came home for lunch every day. However, on the day he killed himself, Mr. P. sat by the window and waved goodbye to his wife when she returned to work after lunch. As she left he said to her, "Be sure my glass is out." He was referring to the only glass his weak hands could still hold.

For years Mr. P. had collected pills for what he called his "suicide kit." Finally, at age 61, he ingested a lethal dose of drugs while his wife was at work. On the way home that evening Mrs. P. sensed her hus-

band would be dead when she arrived. She found Mr.
P. in a coma, with his suicide note nearby, and
quickly summoned two of his physicians. After examining him and taking his medical history into consideration, they decided not to attempt to save his life.
Mrs. P. completely agreed with the doctors' decision.

When Mr. P.'s closest friend found out about the
suicide, he remarked, "I'm only sorry I didn't know he
was trying to kill himself so I could have helped him to
do it."

The second pattern of spouse-assisted suicides involved wives
who discovered their husbands' suicide notes before the self-
inflicted deaths occurred, but failed to take any appropriate action. For example, one woman discovered her husband's suicide
note a week before his death and another the day before the
suicide. In both cases the wives simply refused to believe the
notes pointed to impending danger. It took their husbands'
deaths to convince them.

This second group also included women whose husbands had
told them in advance they were going to kill themselves. In one
case a man told his wife and daughter every night for two weeks
that he wanted to end his life. Because he was an alcoholic his
family doubted his threats were genuine. Thinking he was
merely "crying wolf," they encouraged him to enter an institution for alcoholics. Finally, out of exasperation, he shot himself in
the head.

The third pattern of spouse-assisted suicides also involved
omission rather than comission. Here, the wife's desire for her
husband's death enabled her to procrastinate so long before seeking help that he was dead by the time she finally did. As the
following case history illustrates, not seeking assistance quickly
enough can have as fatal an effect as not seeking help at all.

CASE SEVENTEEN

Mr. Q. awoke early, dressed, and brought in the newspaper. At approximately 8:00 A.M. he ingested a lethal dose of drugs, left a suicide note on his dresser, and went back to sleep while his wife was in the kitchen nearby. Mrs. Q. entered the bedroom several times during the next two hours to tell her husband to get out of bed. However, she said she didn't discover the suicide note until about 10:00 A.M. and didn't take it seriously because her husband was "always talking about how he had lived too long." He was 77 at the time of his death.

One of Mrs. Q.'s friends, who is a nurse, came to visit about 11:00 A.M. Mrs. Q. said she showed her friend the suicide note, but the nurse also discounted its validity.

Mrs. Q. entered the bedroom several times during the next few hours and tried to talk to her husband; however, he did not answer. Although she never attempted to shake him, she said she thought he was sleeping because "he was breathing so normally." Mr. Q. was an unusually poor sleeper and had often needed drugs and/or alcohol to help him to sleep. Mrs. Q. knew her husband had slept soundly the previous night.

Approximately seven hours after she had discovered her husband's suicide note, Mrs. Q. finally called for help. She said she "somehow sensed he was already dead," and she was correct.

Mrs. Q. described her relationship with her husband as so intolerable she had entertained thoughts of "buying a gun and shooting herself on the back lawn." There were numerous violent arguments during their nearly twenty years of marriage, yet they apparently never considered a separation or divorce. When asked if she had ever thought about leaving Mr. Q., she responded, "I felt the Lord would somehow see me through all this." When asked what she regretted most about her husband's suicide, she replied without hesitation, "That he didn't do it sooner."

Mr. Q.'s behavior appears to have been merely a gesture toward suicide. There was little chance he could die as a result of his actions, unless he was certain his wife would "permit him to die."

There are no statistics documenting the actual number of suicides resulting from spouses' inability or unwillingness to initiate appropriate action during a suicidal crisis. Nevertheless, it is reasonable to assume that in any given year there are numerous cases similar to the one cited above in which suicide could not be committed without the full cooperation of a hostile spouse.

Of course, other family members may be unresponsive in situations where relatives are about to kill themselves. Many deaths occur each year because the families of potential suicide victims are inexperienced in dealing with a crisis. They deny the seriousness of the situation and, therefore, are unlikely to recognize and acknowledge the clues given by the relative who is contemplating suicide. The less family reaction the clues generate, the more the potential suicide victim thinks no one cares if he lives or dies, and the sense of futility engendered may convince even the ambivalently suicidal person to take his life.

In late life, clues that indicate intentions of suicide may be as obvious as a suicide attempt, a suicidal threat, a statement of one's desire to die, or a gun purchase, or as subtle as tears for no apparent reason, a changed will, funeral plans made shortly after the death of a loved one, arrangements to donate one's body to science, the giving away of a valued possession, a sudden and unexplainable recovery from a deep depression, the breaking of a long-standing behavioral pattern, or the putting of one's business affairs in order, as though preparation were being made for a long journey. Thousands of lives could be saved each year if people would recognize such clues and then respond to them quickly and appropriately.

In marriages where the wife has been verbally, physically, and emotionally abused by her husband, it is not difficult to understand why she might be in favor of her spouse committing suicide. Wives who stay married to abusive men indicate they do not perceive separation or divorce as acceptable alternatives. It would thus appear that some spouse-assisted suicides may be a substitute means for these wives to obtain the divorce they might have craved, but could never bring themselves to initiate or obtain.[138] Other extremely frustrated wives may assist in their husbands' suicides as a means of obviating the need for their own suicides or murder of their husbands. Therefore, in terms of the psychodynamics of these situations, *the wife who helps her husband to take his life may be attempting to save her own.**

*The dynamics of spouse-assisted suicides are similar when husbands help wives to commit suicide. For additional information on spouse-assisted suicides, consult the following references:[98,103,109,138,143].

14

A Psychological Autopsy of a Geriatric Suicide

The psychological autopsy is a procedure developed at the Los Angeles Suicide Prevention Center as a means of determining the actual mode of death (natural causes, accident, suicide, or homicide) in cases with equivocal circumstances. The technique has been utilized primarily to distinguish suicides from accidental deaths. In order to obtain vital information about a decedent's life, interviews may be conducted with the spouse, siblings, children, parents, other relatives, friends, neighbors, employers, coworkers, physicians, and clergy.

The inquiry, which is often initiated by the county medical examiner's office, is conducted by a team of professionals. Of particular interest to the investigators are events that took place during the final months of the decedent's life. When used in conjunction with the reports of police, pathologists, and the person who discovered the body, the psychological autopsy often results in a reasonably firm conclusion about the actual mode of death. In some cases, peripheral information gathered during the investigation enables survivors to more adequately come to terms with their grief and the complete realization the loved one is dead.

One of the survivors interviewed by the author in Arizona was perplexed by what she perceived as her father's enigmatic suicide. Because of her desire to learn what she could about the events immediately preceding her father's suicide, she became interested in having a psychological autopsy performed. She supplied identifying information that allowed the author to contact people who had detailed knowledge of her father's personal life. The information obtained during the nine-month investigation is presented in Case Eighteen and the discussion that follows the case history.

CASE EIGHTEEN

Although Mr. R. was an unusually healthy man, illness plagued his family all of his life. His mother died in childbirth and his father and grandfather raised him. Because of his wife's medical problems, he moved his family from Alabama to Arizona, where his wife died 19 years later. Mr. R.'s only child was born with birth defects, which eventually required 15 operations. A quiet man who kept to himself, Mr. R. attended church twice weekly and worked for the same company most of his life. He was living with his daughter, who was unmarried and in her thirties, at the time of his suicide.

Because he had paid social security taxes since the program's inception, he was anxious to begin collecting benefits. Against his daughter's advice, he retired at 62 and spent much of his time raising bees, selling honey, and trying to keep busy.

Two months after he retired, he returned to his home town in Alabama for an extended visit. While there he dated the widow of a childhood friend and reached an agreement to marry her. Although he did not give her an engagement ring, it was understood they would marry as soon as he resolved certain problems. Because his fiancee had worked for the same company for 28 years and needed only two additional years to qualify for a pension, she was unable to move from Alabama. They agreed he would maintain his home in Arizona for his daughter after he permanently moved back to Alabama.

Eager to obtain his daughter's opinion of his plans, he called her to discuss his forthcoming marriage and his intention to permanently return to his home town the following spring. His daughter told him she was in favor of the marriage, but made it clear she would remain in Arizona because her home and friends were there. He agreed and said he would join her at the end of the summer.

After he returned home, Mr. R. seemed in very good spirits and continued to write and call his fiancee. However, several people began teasing him about getting married at his age. To cope with their taunts, he began to deny his marital plans to his neighbors, friends, and people he saw at church.

Each day after he retired he continued to visit the company where he had worked. His closest friend at work later indicated "he knew something was wrong with Mr. R., but he couldn't get him to talk about it." His sister called him from the West Coast and said afterwards she knew "something was wrong because he wouldn't let her end the conversation and kept her on the telephone much longer than usual." As time passed, his friends and neighbors began to notice how depressed he was becoming. Therefore, it appears Mr. R. presented several subtle clues to his impending suicide.

As he became more despondent, he confided in his daughter, "I should have never retired because there isn't anything to do. I wish I had never heard the word 'retirement.' " Shortly thereafter he received an unexpected call from his former employer. The company was entering its busy season and wanted him to return to work. He agreed to start working full time the following Monday.

Besides meaning the resumption of meaningful activity, returning to work meant an opportunity to earn more money at a time when financial problems were among his major concerns. More than once he gave his neighbors the impression he had financial difficulties. It appears his financial worries were directly related to providing support for the two women in his life, his daughter and his fiancee. On several occasions Mr. R. had discussed financial considerations with his intended wife and each time they had reached the same conclusion—he wasn't in a position to continue providing support for his daughter and to begin supporting his fiancee.

His home in Arizona still had a mortgage on it and his wife's medical bills had completely depleted his savings. His daughter, who worked part time as a baby-sitter, had taken driving lessons Mr. R. felt were too expensive. He was upset about the possibility he would have to buy his daughter a car if she passed her driving test. These considerations occurred at a time when he was concentrating on decreasing his expenses so he could afford to move back to his home town and remarry. These circumstances appear to have frustrated him and given him a sense of having little control over his life.

Although he opposed using drugs for any reason, he began taking medication for "chest pains caused by tension." The pill prescription was renewed twice during the next year, so it appears Mr. R. had been under stress for more than a year before his suicide. However, after his death, his physician said "suicide seemed totally out of character for Mr. R."

A week before his death, Mr. R. said he was experiencing insomnia and asked his daughter if she had any sleeping pills. She didn't, but suggested his doctor could prescribe some. It had been more than a year since Mr. R. had last been examined by his physician. Mr. R.'s disturbed sleeping pattern was another indication of his suicidal potential.

Three days before his death, Mr. R. hid the key to a storage locker in which he kept honey and instructed his daughter to tell the mailman, who also raised bees, where he had placed the key. His daughter noted the unusual nature of that behavior. With the benefit of hindsight, it now appears leaving the key for the mailman was yet another clue.

On Friday, two days before he killed himself, Mr. R. called his fiancee and told her how depressed he had become. "Nothing is working out. I'm really depressed. I'm going back to work to keep from going stark-raving crazy. I've done everything I could to keep busy, even chopping down a tree. I tried to sell my bees, but nobody wanted to buy them. My daughter passed her driving test and will be wanting a car and I'm worried she'll have a wreck while you and I are living in Alabama."

His fiancee asked him if he had changed his mind about their plans. He insisted he hadn't. "I haven't changed my mind one bit about coming back to you in Alabama. Actually, I'm really sorry I ever came back to Arizona. I'm so tired." She encouraged him to consider his alternatives by reminding him, "There's more than one way to skin a cat." That was their final conversation.

Very early the next morning, a Saturday, Mr. R. insisted his daughter prepare a grocery list so he could go to the supermarket. Such behavior was odd for him because the market wasn't open that early in the morning and he usually wasn't anxious to shop for groceries.

The daughter now suspects he wanted an excuse to leave the house in order to buy shells for his shotgun.

Later that day, his daughter observed Mr. R. rummaging through a strongbox in which he kept his important papers. He discussed auto insurance with her and called their agent to determine if his daughter's coverage could be added to his policy.

Sunday, the morning of his death, he didn't eat breakfast, which was most unusual. He had not eaten much the preceding day, either. Although he said he didn't feel well enough to go to church with his daughter, he insisted he drive her there. The church was only three blocks from their home.

After driving his daughter to church, he came home and placed his wallet, keys, and an address book in one of her desk drawers. His wallet contained $300, an enormous amount of cash for him to have been carrying. He then locked their dog in his bedroom, which was also unusual, since the family had always locked the dog in the daughter's room. He went into the den, took off his shoes, and using his toes to pull the trigger of his shotgun, shot himself in the chest. His body was discovered by his daughter when she returned from church.

The following morning two letters arrived from his fiancee. The daughter read them and described them as "merely friendly with no romantic overtones." The fiancee never wrote or called again and the daughter made no attempt to contact her.

Comments on Case Eighteen

It seems apparent Mr. R. was depressed by much more than his self-imposed retirement because he committed suicide the day before he was scheduled to return to work. There is no indication he would have had to "swallow his pride" in order to return to work, because the company had urged him to come out of retirement.

His daughter wondered why he killed himself on Sunday, when he was alone Friday and Saturday nights until midnight. First, it is unlikely he purchased the shotgun shells until Saturday morning. Second, he may not have wanted his daughter to find his body while she was alone. He knew she'd be alone when returning from work on Friday and Saturday nights, but he may have hoped someone would have driven her home from church on Sunday and come in for a visit. (Someone did drive her home, but didn't come into the house with her). Third, Mr. R. was a deeply religious man and may have wanted driving his daughter to church to be the final act he would perform for her.

His daughter speculated that one of the most depressing aspects of her father's life was being a widower. She spoke of her parents' closeness and her father's shock when her mother died of a heart attack. However, Mrs. R. had been quite ill for some time and an invalid for at least the last year of her life. Furthermore, Mr. R. didn't exhibit the typical manifestations of protracted grief. Rather than brooding about the past, he was in the process of remarrying and establishing a new life style for himself. Also, his kin in Alabama strongly supported his forthcoming marriage. His relatives apparently felt he had spent his entire adult life working to pay his family's medical bills and deserved a respite during his later years. Therefore, it does not appear that being a widower was deleteriously affecting Mr. R. shortly before his suicide.

Ironically, while talking with his relatives in Alabama, the subject of suicide had been discussed. Mr. R. emphatically stated he felt "suicide was wrong." However, as has often been noted in the literature, what people say about death before they face it may have little relevance to how they will act when placed under inordinate stress and/or pain.

One puzzling aspect of this case is: why did Mr. R. chose to kill himself on the day before he was to return to work if he were so disenchanted with retirement? The question is deceptively simple because it suggests that returning to work would have been a panacea for him. Actually, returning to work may have presented other problems which were not so readily apparent.

One of his most revealing statements was: "I'm so tired." The suicidal elderly will sometimes talk about feeling tired not to describe a physical condition, but rather a state of "psychological exhaustion." These people have typically grown tired of facing the myriad day-to-day problems of living in our complex society. After having worked all his life to pay so many medical bills, and having so little materially to show for his labor, Mr. R. may have been profoundly overwhelmed by the prospect of "starting from scratch" again. A late-life attempt at building financial security for the two women he cared for may have appeared to him a much greater responsibility than he could possibly bear under the circumstances.

Mr. R.'s fiancee felt his distorted perception of his financial problems was the primary etiological factor. In reality his financial problems were certainly not severe. He received social security benefits; his daughter worked part time; he could have given her his car rather than buy another one; his daughter could have found a roommate to help pay for household expenses (as she did after her father's death); Mr. R. could have moved into his fiancee's house in Alabama; and his fiancee would have begun receiving a pension in less than two years. In the meantime, she had her own source of income.

It is clear that Mr. R.'s financial problems were not very serious. What is not so easily understood is the illogic of the suicidal mind. Circular logic and dichotomous logic are the hallmarks of impaired suicidal reasoning. Asked why he is thinking of taking his life, a potential suicide replies "Because my problems are insurmountable." Asked how he knows his problems are insurmountable, he responds, "Are you kidding, if my problems weren't insurmountable, do you think I'd be on the verge of killing myself?" Such a statement is typical of the potential suicide's circular logic.

It is also common for the suicidal mind to approach a dilemma by means of a "black or white evaluation." Thus, the dichotomous logic of the potential suicide may reason, "If my life can't be perfect (exactly as I want it to be), then I must end it." Gradations between polar extremes are usually not perceived by the suicidal mind—no gray is seen between the black and white.

Conclusions on Case Eighteen

Several suicidogenic forces simultaneously impinged on Mr. R. and each appears to have diminished the quality of his life. However, if any one factor was especially harmful, it appears to have been his inability—characteristic of the suicidal person—to perceive alternatives. By focusing on the black-or-white dichotomy of "perfect life versus death," the potential suicide further diminishes the chances of positively resolving his problems.

Mr. R. had painted himself into a corner and could no longer see the center of the room, the windows, or the door. Because he couldn't see a way out of his predicament, his only alternative was to escape through death.

If Mr. R. could have reduced his self-imposed burden into "bite-sized problems," there is every reason to believe he could have resolved them one at a time and continued to live. This seems to be a particularly reasonable assumption given the support and concern of his daughter and fiancee. However, it appears he no longer had the ego strength required to successfully cope with such severe stress. His fiancee's observation, "there is more than one way to skin a cat," may have been the most valuable advice he ever received, but unfortunately, he was unable to act on it.

Mr. R. was the victim of a dilemma he created. He had crossed the line that for each person separates the amount of stress that can and cannot be tolerated. Once his "line of unbearability" had been crossed, he no longer had to decide what to do because in his mind suicide became his only alternative.

15

How We Can Decrease the Number of Geriatric Suicides

As long as there are extremely unhappy, depressed, alienated, frustrated, ailing, debilitated, and deranged people, suicides will continue to be committed, no matter what we do to try to prevent them. In light of this fact of life, perhaps the name of our goal should be "suicide reduction" rather than "suicide prevention." Success or failure could be measured by the fluctuation of suicide rates, and no one could get the idea that we actually expect, or even want, to prevent all suicides.

Looking at the different approaches to preventative efforts conducted through the years, one could easily get the impression that suicide cannot be prevented. We certainly have not succeeded in lowering suicide rates in the United States. However, unless one equates suicide prevention with the complete elimination of suicide, there is much that can be done to lower suicide rates.

In order to substantially reduce the number of suicides committed in our country, we first need a firm national commitment to suicide reduction as one of our major mental health priorities. The President, the Secretary of Health, Education and Welfare, the Director of the National Institute of Mental Health, or someone else of authority would need to espouse and articulate such a goal and be prepared to support its achievement with adequate funding. The concerted, closely coordinated efforts of numerous public and private organizations would become the next logical step.

In the hope such a commitment will ultimately be forthcoming, the following suggestions are offered as a means of substantially lowering the suicide rates associated with older people. Naturally, other steps would be necessary to seriously reduce the number of suicides among younger populations.

Retirement. (1) Allow people who want to continue working beyond retirement age to do so as long as they can physically and mentally perform adequately on the job.

(2) People who want to stop working at a given age could be eased into retirement. Three or four years before retiring, they would begin to work fewer hours each year, thus cushioning the blow of retirement shock.

(3) Preretirement education and counseling could be given to employees far in advance of the time they actually stop working.

(4) Postretirement counseling could be provided for at least the first two years after employment has ceased.

Physicians. (5) Physicians, particularly family physicians, geriatricians, and psychiatrists, could be taught how to recognize and appropriately respond to the "clues to suicide" their older patients present. Suicide intervention training for physicians could be provided in the nation's medical schools, during internships and residencies, or through continuing education programs.

(6) Free annual medical examinations provided for everyone 60 and older would not only help to detect serious illness before it's too late to be treated, but would also increase the frequency of contacts with professional people. If those professionals were properly trained, they could have more opportunities to detect suicidal symptoms.

(7) The recently bereaved need to have their physical condi-

tion very closely monitored during the first year of bereavement because morbidity and mortality rates are so elevated during that period.

Family and Friends. (8) Closer family ties and increased dosages of tender loving care and touching would definitely be a step in the right direction.

(9) Breaking down the ingrained taboo against sexuality in later life could reduce frustration and promote mental, emotional, and physical health.

Public and Private Agencies. (10) Suicide prevention centers and mental health centers could institute outreach programs to identify and treat potentially suicidal older people. Meaningful roles and part-time employment opportunities for the aged would be ancillary benefits of using the elderly as outreach workers.

(11) Access to reasonably priced psychiatric and psychological services is vital. Accessibility also includes low-cost transportation (for example, Dial-a-Ride).

Society. (12) The pervasive stigma associated with mental health care (especially for men) needs to be acknowledged, confronted, and mitigated.

(13) In a very general and basic sense, there needs to be a much greater awareness of the problems associated with growing old in our country. Without that sensitivity, there will probably never be any commitment to significantly decreasing the number of older people who kill themselves in the United States each year.

Telephone Companies. (14) No older person who is living alone should be without a telephone, which can be the link to many necessary services. Telephone companies could install telephones free of charge for those people and lower their monthly charges for basic service.

(15) Free stickers with the phone numbers of local helpful and vital services could be widely distributed to older people so that they could affix them to their telephones.

Government. (16) Telephone reassurance, information and referral, and crisis intervention services could be explained to older people through the use of flyers included with their social security checks.

(17) Research funds could be allocated to study the problem of geriatric suicides. Any serious intervention program, particularly one that is national in scope, needs a consistent infusion of funds in order to reach its goal.

National Organizations. (18) A national program to inhibit suicide among the elderly would benefit from the endorsement and cooperation of large organizations of older people (such as the American Association of Retired Persons), unions, churches, etc.

Media. (19) A national public information campaign could be launched to familiarize people with the "clues to suicide" much in the way the "warning signs of cancer" were publicized.

(20) Magazines read primarily by older people (such as *Modern Maturity, Dynamic Maturity, Retirement Living*) could publish articles about geriatric suicides, which they have not been willing to do in the past.

Research. (21) More meaningful leisure and recreational activities for mature adults must be identified and created. A steady diet of shuffleboard and checkers will not sustain an active mind or body for long. Research on the subject of enriching and fulfilling activities for people with much free time could benefit large numbers of older and handicapped people.

(22) Greater attention could be focused on the special needs of widows and widowers. Research could determine if there are unusually helpful coping styles to help in the resolution of grief reactions. If there are, and they can be taught, "well-adjusted" widows and widowers could teach effective coping strategies to the recently bereaved.

(23) A simple means of early detection of high suicidal potential in a given aged population would be extremely useful. One approach would be the continued development of profiles of the "typical older suicidal person."[38] As the profiles become refined to the point where they are truly predictive, and not merely descriptive, they could be used to identify high suicidal risk by those who contact large groups of older people (such as employees of senior centers). Special intervention techniques could then be used to identify and assist people who are at greatest risk.

Appendix

A Review of the Research on Geriatric Suicide

        Although the problem of suicide among the elderly is serious, a comparatively small number of studies has investigated the phenomenon. A literature search yielded 19 studies available in English, which have been summarized in the following pages. Several articles in other languages were not taken into consideration in this total, although they have been included in the bibliography.

    The earliest of the 19 studies looked at geriatric suicides in a Danish psychiatric hospital,[28] while the most recently conducted research examined older white males in Arizona.[35] The number of older subjects studied was as small as 1[23] and as large as 301,[35] while the ages of the subjects were as low as 45[48] and as high as 90.[24] In reporting the results of 5 of the investigations, the authors neglected to state the period under study,[43,45,48,59,60] while 2 researchers did not provide a male/female breakdown of their samples.[2,59]

    In 2 of the studies the subjects were institutionalized before or during their suicidal episodes,[28,60] a factor which limits generalizability to the noninstitutionalized elderly. Five of the investigations focused on the suicidal behavior of older psychiatric patients,[21,28,43,48,60] thereby detracting from their generalizability to the vast majority of elderly who are not psychiatric patients.

By not segregating their subjects by age, 5 studies did not distinguish between the "young old" and the "old old,"[2,11,44,59,60] One investigation only asked men aged 45 to 65 about their "suicidal ideas and previous suicidal behavior."[48] It would appear this study was actually examining mostly middle-aged rather than elderly men as purported.

Ten studies were researched in other countries,[28,45,59] including 4 in England,[2,6,14,50] 2 in Scotland,[5,44] and 1 in Ireland.[57] The conclusions reached by those foreign studies may also have only limited generalizability to older suicides in the United States; however, they certainly illustrate the international nature of the geriatric suicide problem.

A Summary of the Research on Suicide among the Elderly

In the summary of research that follows, the key to abbreviations used is found on each page.

R: Barraclough, B. M. *Y:* 1971 *S:* 30 *L:* England *M/F:* not stated *A:* 65+ *C:* no

Abstract: A retrospective examination of all consecutive suicide completions in the County of West Sussex and the Borough of Portsmouth during December 1, 1967 through January 31, 1969. The most prominent symptoms observed were: mood change, insomnia, weight loss, hypochondriasis, guilt, difficulty concentrating, anxiety, and agitation.

Key: R: Researcher(s); *Y:* Year of Publication; *S:* Size of Aged Suicide Sample; *L:* Location of Research; *M/F:* Male/Female Breakdown; *A:* Age Breakdown; *C:* Use of a Control Group

R: Batchelor, I. R. C.; Napier, Margaret Y: 1953 S: 40 L: Scotland M/F: 16 m; 24 f A: 60+ C: no

Abstract: A follow-up study of consecutive cases of attempted suicides admitted to a general hospital in Edinburgh during 1950 through 1952. The most common factors observed were: morbid sensitivity, seclusiveness, obsessional disposition, few friends, loneliness, mental illness, depression, insomnia, anorexia, hypochondrias, confusion, and fatigue.

R: Bean, Philip Y: 1973 S: 67 L: England M/F: 21 m; 46 f A: 60+ C: no

Abstract: A comparison of 44 accidental self-poisonings with 67 intentional self-poisonings among patients admitted to 1 of 3 general hospitals in the Chichester section of Sussex during 1967 through 1971. All 111 cases of self-poisoning among the elderly were compared with 824 cases of self-poisoning among people aged 10 through 59. Results showed that accident victims had a lower death rate, but had taken a much wider range of drugs. However, in a number of other respects, the populations were similar. These results, although inconclusive, suggested that perhaps the accident victims and the attempted suicides should be seen as separate groups.

R: Bock, E. Wilbur; Webber, Irving Y: 1972 S: 188 L: Florida M/F: 147 m; 41 f A: 65+ C: yes

Abstract: A comparison of 1,246 nonsuicidal males with 147 male suicides and 1,298 nonsuicidal females with 41 female suicides in Pinellas County during 1955 through 1963. All geriatric suicide cases in the county were included. Found that: (1) the widowed exhibit higher suicide rates than the married; (2) this differential is partially explained by the greater social isolation of the widowed, particularly the widowers; (3) the widowed can find in other types of relationships meaningful alternatives to marriage

Key: R: Researcher(s); Y: Year of Publication; S: Size of Aged Suicide Sample; L: Location of Research; M/F: Male/Female Breakdown; A: Age Breakdown; C: Use of a Control Group that help prevent suicidal behavior; (4) widowers have greater difficulty than widows in making effective substitutions for the loss of spouse; and (5) there appear to be limits to the effective mitigation of these alternatives for the widowed, especially the widower.

R: Burston, G. R.   *Y:* 1969   *S:* 33   *L:* England   *M/F:* 8 m; 25 f
A: 65+ m; 60+ f *C:* no

Abstract: Limited to cases of self-poisoning. Compared 33 geriatric suicide attempters with a combined total of 472 male and female suicide attempters. Males were aged 12 through 64 and females were aged 12 through 59. All had been admitted to the Sunderland District Poisoning Treatment Centre during October 1, 1966 through March 31, 1968. Self-poisoning in elderly patients appears more deliberate and is usually more efficiently carried out than it is in younger patients. Some episodes of geriatric self-poisoning among those who are chronically ill appear to be an attempt to avoid an unpleasant impending death.

R: Gardner, Elmer; Bahn, Anita; Mack, Marjorie *Y:* 1964 *S:* 75
L: New York *M/F:* 55 m; 20 f *A:* 55+ *C:* no

Abstract: Examined completed suicides in Monroe County during 1960 through 1962 to determine how many had previous psychiatric treatment. Showed that the diagnosis of psychotic or neurotic depression was related to a suicide rate of 551 per 100,000 in those over 55, compared with 159 per 100,000 for those under 55. Noted that although the rate of attempted suicide is relatively low in old as compared to younger people, an attempt that had occurred in late life portended successful suicide, usually within the first year after the attempt.

R: Haggerty, Judith *Y:* 1973 *S:* 1 *L:* Massachusetts *M/F:* 1 m
A: 70 *C:* no

Key: R: Researcher(s); *Y:* Year of Publication; *S:* Size of Aged Suicide Sample;
L: Location of Research; *M/F:* Male/Female Breakdown; *A:* Age Breakdown; *C:* Use
of a Control Group

Abstract: In-depth examination of a 70-year-old widower who attempted suicide 3 times in 4 months during early 1971. The author, a psychiatric social worker, expressed her fear that the man would again resort to suicidal behavior the next time he experienced depression and a major loss.

R: Hickman, Jack *Y:* 1965 *S:* 4 *L:* Indiana *M/F:* 3 m; 1 f *A:* 80+ *C:* no

Abstract: A discussion of 4 cases of attempted suicides among older people seen at Marion County General Hospital during 1950 through 1964. Included a report on a 90-year-old man who attempted suicide because he feared impending blindness and subsequent dependence on his wife. Described factors that may alert a physician to possible suicide attempts among older patients.

R: Kiørboe, Erik *Y:* 1951 *S:* 35 *L:* Denmark *M/F:* 25 m; 10 f *A:* 60+ *C:* no

Abstract: A review of the case histories of 35 residents of De Gamles By Psychiatric Hospital in Copenhagen. The suicides were attempted or completed during 1939 through 1948. Motives for the geriatric suicides were seen as: physical discomfort, mental changes, alcoholism, and syphilis. Concluded marital conflicts, economic insecurity, and loneliness were rarely associated with the suicides studied.

R: MacMahon, Brian; Pugh, Thomas *Y:* 1965 *S:* 229 *L:* Massachusetts *M/F:* 155 m; 74 f *A:* 50+ *C:* yes

Abstract: A comparison of widowed people who committed suicide with widowed people who died of other causes during 1948 through 1952. Deaths from suicide clustered in the first four years of widowhood, but were especially noticeable in the first year. The relative risk of suicide was estimated to be 2.5 times higher

Key: R: Researcher(s); *Y:* Year of Publication; *S:* Size of Aged Suicide Sample; *L:* Location of Research; *M/F:* Male/Female Breakdown; *A:* Age Breakdown; *C:* Use of a Control Group

in the first year after the death of the spouse, and 1.5 times higher in the second, third, and fourth years, than after the fourth year.

R: Miller, Marv *Y:* 1976 *S:* 301 *L:* Arizona *M/F:* 301 m *A:* 60+ *C:* yes

Abstract: An analysis of white male suicides committed during January 1, 1970 through December 31, 1975. Included a comparison of 30 male suicides with a matched control group of men who died of natural causes in Maricopa County. Resulted in a profile of a typical male geriatric suicide. Found 62 percent of the suicides were related to serious physical illness. Retirement had an adverse effect on many of the suicides, and 60 percent of the men gave verbal or behavioral clues to their impending lethal behavior.

R: O'Neal, Patricia; Robins, Eli; Schmidt, Edwin *Y:* 1956 *S:* 19 *L:* Missouri *M/F:* 14 m; 5 f *A:* 60+ *C:* no

Abstract: A comparison of 19 older psychiatric patients who attempted suicide in St. Louis with 90 patients aged 59 and younger who also attempted. The period under study and the name of the hospital were not given. Determined that every older suicidal patient had an evident psychiatric illness before the attempt. About 90 percent of the sample had a psychotic illness (chronic brain syndrome, acute brain syndrome, or psychotic depression).

R: Proudfoot, A. T.; Wright, N. *Y:* 1972 *S:* 131 *L:* Scotland *M/F:* 38 m; 93 f *A:* 65+ *C:* no

Abstract: A comparison of 131 older patients with 965 patients aged 64 and younger, all of whom poisoned themselves. The subjects were patients of the Regional Poisoning Treatment

Key: R: Researcher(s); Y: Year of Publication; S: Size of Aged Suicide Sample; L: Location of Research; M/F: Male/Female Breakdown; A: Age Breakdown; C: Use of a Control Group

Centre of the Royal Infirmary in Edinburgh during 1967 through 1969. Concluded that the elderly are not more likely to die as a result of self-poisoning than younger people, although the incidence of complications was greater in the older group.

R: Quidu, M. *Y:* 1969 *S:* 27 *L:* France *M/F:* 13 m; 14 f *A:* 55+ *C:* no

Abstract: A comparison of 25 older patients who attempted suicide with 47 patients aged 15 through 25 who also attempted. The period under study was not given. Noted that ⅔ of older suicidal patients studied presented psychiatric problems. The other third of the attempts occurred when a relatively harmless difficulty beset someone who was affected by a recent frustrating event. For men the event was usually the onset of severe physical illness. For women it was frequently the mourning of a child's departure.

R: Robins, Lee; West, Patricia; Murphy, George *Y:* 1977 *S:* 104 *L:* Missouri *M/F:* 104 m *A:* 45–65 *C:* yes

Abstract: A comparison of white and black psychiatric and medical patients of Malcolm Bliss Hospital in St. Louis with a matched control group. Limited to lower-class men aged 65 and younger. The period under study was not stated. Six variables were found to distinguish suicidal from nonsuicidal patients and whites from blacks: (1) social integration; (2) knowledge of or relation to a suicide attempter or completer; (3) attitude toward aging; (4) secular attitudes; (5) brain damage from alcohol; and (6) depressive illness.

R: Sainsbury, Peter *Y:* 1955 *S:* 173 *L:* England *M/F:* 116 m; 57 f *A:* 55+ *C:* no

Abstract: An analysis of social and demographic variables related to suicides in North London during 1936 through 1938, which

Key: *R:* Researcher(s); *Y:* Year of Publication; *S:* Size of Aged Suicide Sample; *L:* Location of Research; *M/F:* Male/Female Breakdown; *A:* Age Breakdown; *C:* Use of a Control Group were used to validate correlated suicide rates in 28 metropolitan boroughs and London during 1929 through 1933. Reviewed the evidence that associated suicide with sex, age, marital status, and various indices of social isolation. Concluded that social factors clearly relate in a predictable way to the incidence of suicide in a community, although that doesn't mean that social factors are causes.

R: Walsh, Dermot; McCarthy, P. Desmond *Y:* 1965 *S:* 90 *L:* Ireland *M/F:* 54 m; 36 f *A:* 60+ *C:* no

Abstract: A statistical and demographic study of suicide among Dublin's elderly during 1954 through 1963, which included geriatric suicide rates of several countries for 1956 through 1958. Indicated that 55.5 percent of the sample had seen a physician within 3 months of their suicides. In 12.2 percent of the cases, the doctor was a psychiatrist.

R: Wiendieck, Gerd *Y:* 1970 *S:* 56 *L:* Germany *M/F:* not stated *A:* 65+ *C:* no

Abstract: Employed a questionnaire to elicit data on the suicidal thoughts of randomly selected people whose average age was 73. The period under study and the sex of the respondents was not stated. About 20 percent of those questioned reported having suicidal thoughts. Others expressed feelings of loneliness, resignation, and being tired of living. Life satisfaction was significantly lower in people with suicidal thoughts.

R: Wolff, Kurt *Y:* 1969 *S:* 100 *L:* Pennsylvania *M/F:* 100 m *A:* 60+ *C:* yes

Abstract: A comparison of 100 depressed nonsuicidal male patients of the Veterans Administration Hospital in Coatesville with an equal number of psychotically depressed suicidal male patients. The period under study was not given. In the nonsuici-

Key: R: Researcher(s); *Y:* Year of Publication; *S:* Size of Aged Suicide Sample; *L:* Location of Research; *M/F:* Male/Female Breakdown; *A:* Age Breakdown; *C:* Use of a Control Group

dal group, depression was related to failure or loss of: physical health, independence, social status, a spouse or close relative. In the suicidal group, depression was related to compulsive behavior associated with work, ambition, and perfection.

Three studies were limited to cases of self-poisoning,[6,14,44] another to suicidal behavior among widows and widowers,[33] and seven others to suicide attempts rather than completions.[5,14,23,24,43,45,60] Some confusion still exists about whether those who attempt suicide comprise a population distinct from those who complete suicide; however, it appears these two populations are much more similar among the elderly than they are among younger people.[15]

Perhaps the most serious deficiency of the research on geriatric suicide is that only 5 of the 19 studies included control groups. Without control groups it cannot be determined which behavior is associated with geriatric suicide and which is merely indicative of old age per se. Such a distinction is crucial to an incisive understanding of the dynamics of suicide in late life, since the overwhelming majority of the aged do not take their own lives.

None of the investigations of geriatric suicides has satisfactorily explained why there are so many male suicides in late life. As mentioned in Chapter 1, Busse and Pfeiffer noted that depression, the mental state most frequently associated with successful suicides in old age, is at least as common among women as it is among men.[15] They speculated that the impact of retirement, physical decline, and/or illness is more damaging to the self-esteem of older men than to older women.

One investigator enumerated and described various patterns of older white male suicides and suggested they occurred as demonstrative reactions to adverse aspects of the geriatric suicides' lives.[35] Unfortunately, the study on which this work was based did not include women, so it is not known if similar patterns could also be observed in a population of older female suicides.

Suggestions for Further Research

Research in the future should concentrate on a unified multistate effort to study suicide among the elderly rather than continue to produce fragmented approaches to the problem. For example, research could be conducted concurrently in the nine states where more than half of the nation's older people reside (California, Florida, Illinois, Michigan, New Jersey, New York, Ohio, Pennsylvania, and Texas). A less ambitious project could examine geriatric suicides in California, New York, and Pennsylvania, where a quarter of the elderly live.

One important aspect of geriatric suicide yet to be investigated is suicide among older women. No study has specifically examined female geriatric suicides, although MacMahon and Pugh did comment on the suicides of 74 women aged 50 and older in their study of suicide among widows and widowers.[33] The need for research on older women who commit suicide is definitely indicated.

Questions to Be Answered by Future Research

Before we may truly speak of suicide prevention among the elderly, we will first need to answer these questions:

1. How can we help physicians to more easily recognize and treat the older suicidal patient?
2. How can we reach out into the community to accurately identify the older suicidal person?
3. How can we provide psychiatric and psychological services for older men without stigmatizing them as being weak?
4. How can we make psychiatric and psychological services more affordable and accessible to older people?

5. How can we help middle-aged wives to recognize the clues to the suicidal behavior presented by so many husbands as they grow older?

6. How can we ameliorate the insidious and often deleterious effects of retirement?

7. How can we forge more meaningful social roles and recreational activities in late life?

8. Are there important differences between suicides among older men and older women?

9. Which coping styles are the most effective for widows and widowers who want to resolve their grief reactions?

10. Can effective coping styles be taught to the about-to-be or recently bereaved?

11. Would stricter gun control help prevent suicide among older men?

12. Should we attempt to prevent all cases of suicide among the elderly, including those that involve euthanasia?

Conclusions on the Research to Date

Older Americans are grossly overrepresented among the nation's suicide victims, yet this problem has basically been neglected by the majority of suicidological and gerontological research in the United States. Only nine studies of the problem have been conducted in our country. In general, the research on geriatric suicides has been fragmented, uncoordinated, noncomparable, and, for the most part, lacking in control groups. Thus, vital questions remain to be answered before geriatric suicides may be prevented to any significant degree.

Bibliography

1. Atkinson, Maxwell. "The Samaritans and the Elderly." In *Proceedings of the Fifth International Conference for Suicide* (Richard Fox, ed.). London, September 24–27, 1969, pp. 159–166.

2. Barraclough, B. M. "Suicide in the Elderly." In *Recent Developments in Psychogeriatrics* (D. W. Kay & A. Walk, eds.). Kent, Eng.: Headly Brothers, 1971, pp. 89–97.

3. Batchelor, I.R.C. "Management and Prognosis of Suicidal Attempts in Old Age." *Geriatrics* 10:291–293 (1955).

4. Batchelor, I. R. C. "Suicide in Old Age." In *Clues to Suicide* (E. Shneidman & N. Farberow, eds.). New York: McGraw-Hill, 1957, pp. 143–152.

5. Batchelor, I. R. C. & Napier, Margaret. "Attempted Suicide in Old Age." *British Medical Journal* 2:1186–1190 (1953).

6. Bean, Philip. "Accidental and Intentional Self-poisoning in the Over-60 Age Group." *Gerontologia Clinica* 15:259–267 (1973).

7. Bennett, A. E. "Recognizing the Potential Suicide." *Geriatrics* 22:175–181 (May 1967).

8. Benson, Roger & Brodie, Donald. "Suicide by Overdoses of Medicines among the Aged." *Journal of the American Geriatrics Society* 23:304–308 (July 1975).

9. Birren, James. *The Psychology of Aging.* Englewood Cliffs: Prentice-Hall, 1964, pp. 258–260.

10. Bock, E. Wilbur. "Aging and Suicide." *The Family Coordinator* 21:71–79 (January 1972).

11. Bock, E. Wilbur & Webber, Irving. "Suicide Among the Elderly." *Journal of Marriage and the Family* 34:24–31 (February 1972).

12. Botwinick, Jack. *Aging and Behavior.* 2nd ed. New York: Springer, 1978, Chapter 3.

13. Bromley, D. B. *The Psychology of Human Ageing.* Baltimore: Penguin, 1966, pp. 125–126, 135, 139–140, 144.

14. Burston, G. R. "Self-poisoning in Elderly Patients." *Gerontologia Clinica* 11:279–289 (1969).

15. Busse, Ewald & Pfeiffer, Eric. *Behavior and Adaptation in Late Life.* Boston: Little, Brown, 1969, pp. 212–213, 221–224.

16. Butler, Robert & Lewis, Myrna. *Aging and Mental Health.* St. Louis: Mosby, 1973, pp. 61–64.

17. Farberow, Norman & Moriwaki, Sharon. "Self-destructive Crises in the Older Person." *The Gerontologist* 15:333–337 (August 1975).

18. Farberow, Norman & Shneidman, Edwin. "Suicide and Age." In *The Psychology of Suicide* (E. Shneidman et al., eds.). New York: Science House, 1970, pp. 165–174.

19. Friedeman, Joyce. "Cry for Help: Suicide in the Aged." *Journal of Gerontological Nursing* 2:28–32 (May–June 1976).

20. Gage, Frances. "Suicide in the Aged." *American Journal of Nursing* 71:2153–2155 (November 1971).

21. Gardner, Elmer, Bahn, Anita, & Mack, Marjorie. "Suicide and Psychiatric Care in the Aging." *Archives of General Psychiatry* 10:547–553 (June 1964).

22. Grollman, Earl. *Suicide: Prevention, Intervention, and Postvention*. Boston: Beacon Press, 1971, pp. 57–58, 132–134.

23. Haggerty, Judith. "Suicidal Behavior in a 70-year-old Man." *Journal of Geriatric Psychiatry* 6:43–51 (1973).

24. Hickman, Jack. "Attempted Suicide in the Aged." *Journal of the Indiana State Medical Association* 58:1138–1140 (1965).

25. Kahne, Merton et al. "Discussion: Suicide in the Aging." *Journal of Geriatric Psychiatry* 6:52–69 (1973).

26. Kastenbaum, Robert & Aisenberg, Ruth. "Suicide and Age." In *The Psychology of Death*. New York: Springer, 1972, pp. 252–254.

27. Kimmel, Douglas. *Adulthood and Aging*. New York: Wiley, 1974, pp. 326–328.

28. Kiørboe, Erik. "Suicide and Attempted Suicide Among Old People." *Journal of Gerontology* 6:233–236 (1951).

29. Labovitz, Sanford. "Variations in Suicide Rates (by Age)." In *Suicide* (Jack Gibbs, ed.). New York: Harper & Row, 1968, p. 65.

30. Lester, David. "Suicide, Homicide, and Age Dependency Ratios." *International Journal of Aging and Human Development* 4:127–132 (Spring 1973).

31. Lettieri, Dan. "Empirical Prediction of Suicidal Risk Among the Aging." *Journal of Geriatric Psychiatry* 6:7–42 (1973).

32. Leviton, Dan. "The Significance of Sexuality as a Deterrent to Suicide among the Aged." *Omega* 4:163–174 (Summer 1973).

33. MacMahon, Brian & Pugh, Thomas. "Suicide in the Widowed." *American Journal of Epidemiology* 81:23–31 (1965).

34. Maris, Ronald. "Age and the Suicide Rate." In *Social Forces in Urban Suicide*. Homewood, Ill.: Dorsey Press, 1969, pp. 93–96, 98–100.

35. Miller, Marv. *Suicide among Older Men*. Doctoral dissertation, The University of Michigan, 1976.

36. Miller, Marv. "Surviving the Loss of a Loved One." *Thanatos* 2:14–18 (June 1977).

37. Miller, Marv. "The Physician and the Older Suicidal Patient." *The Journal of Family Practice* 5:1028–1029 (December 1977).

38. Miller, Marv. "Toward a Profile of the Older White Male Suicide." *The Gerontologist* 18:80–82 (February 1978).

39. Miller, Marv. "A Psychological Autopsy of a Geriatric Suicide." *Journal of Geriatric Psychiatry* 10:229–242 (March 1978).

40. Miller, Marv. "Geriatric Suicide: The Arizona Study." *The Gerontologist* 18:488–495 (October 1978).

41. Niccolini, Robert. "Reading the Signals for Suicidal Risk." *Geriatrics* 28:71–72 (May 1973).

42. Niswander, G. D., Casey, T. & Humphrey, J. "Elderly Sick Suicide." In *A Panorama of Suicide* (G. D. Niswander et al., eds.). Springfield, Ill.: Charles R. Thomas, 1973, pp. 117–125.

43. O'Neal, Patricia, Robins, Eli & Schmidt, Edwin. "A Psychiatric Study of Attempted Suicide in Persons over Sixty Years of Age." *A.M.A. Archives of Neurology and Psychiatry* 75:275–284 (1956).

44. Proudfoot, A. T. & Wright, N. "The Physical Consequences of Self-poisoning by the Elderly." *Gerontologia Clinica* 14:25–31 (1972).

45. Quidu, M. "Suicide Attempts in Adolescents and the Elderly." In *Proceedings of the Fifth International Conference for Suicide Prevention* (Richard Fox, ed.). London, September 24–27, 1969, pp. 37–40.

46. Rachlis, David. "Suicide and Loss Adjustment in the Aging." *Bulletin of Suicidology* O:23–26 (Fall 1970).

47. Resnik, H. L. P. & Cantor, Joel. "Suicide and Aging." *Journal of the American Geriatrics Society* 18:152–158 (1970).

48. Robins, Lee, West, Patricia & Murphy, George. "The High Rate of Suicide in Older White Men." *Social Psychiatry* 12:1–20 (1977).

49. Roth, Martin. "Suicide in Old Age." *Canada's Mental Health* 11:27 (1963).

50. Sainsbury, Peter. *Suicide in London: An Ecological Study.* London: Chapman & Hall, 1955.

51. Sainsbury, Peter. "Suicide in Old Age." *Proceedings of the Royal Society of Medicine* 54:266–268 (1961).

52. Sainsbury, Peter. "Suicide in Later Life." *Gerontologia Clinica* 4:161–170 (1962).

53. Sainsbury, Peter. "Suicide in the Middle and Later Years." In *Medical and Clinical Aspects of Aging* (H. T. Blumenthal, ed.). New York: Columbia University Press, 1962, pp. 97–105.

54. Sainsbury, Peter. "Social and Epidemiological Aspects of Suicide with Special Reference to the Aged." In *Processes of Aging: Social and Psychological Perspectives* (R. H. Williams et al., eds.). New York: Atherton Press, 1963, pp. 153–175.

55. Shneidman, Edwin. "Suicide in the Aged." In *The Doctor and the Dying Patient* (Richard Davis, ed.). Los Angeles: Andrus Gerontology Center, 1971, pp. 1–6.

56. Stengel, Erwin. *Suicide and Attempted Suicide.* Baltimore: Penguin, 1964, p. 27.

57. Walsh, Dermot & McCarthy, P. Desmond. "Suicide in Dublin's Elderly." *Acta Psychiatrica Scandanavica* 41:227–235 (1965).

58. Weiss, James. "Suicide in the Aged." In *Suicidal Behaviors: Diagnosis and Management* (H. L. P. Resnik, ed.). Boston: Little, Brown, 1968, pp. 255–267.

59. Wiendieck, Gerd. "Social Determinants of Suicide in Old Age." In *Proceedings of the Fifth International Conference for Suicide Prevention* (Richard Fox, ed.). London, September 24–27, 1969, pp. 196–197.

60. Wolff, Kurt. "Depression and Suicide in the Geriatric Patient." *Journal of the American Geriatrics Society* 17:668–672 (July 1969).

61. Wolff, Kurt. "Observations on Depression and Suicide in the Geriatric Patient." In *Patterns of Self-destruction* (Kurt Wolff, ed.). Springfield, Ill.: Charles R. Thomas, 1970, pp. 33–42.

62. Wolff, Kurt. "The Treatment of the Depressed and Suicidal Geriatric Patient." *Geriatrics* 26:65–69 (July 1971).

63. "Suicide Patterns in the Elderly." *Geriatrics* 22:68 (1967).

64. "Lonely Golden Agers may be Suicidal." *Today's Health* 51:8 (June 1973).

Hard-to-Find and Foreign Language References

65. Atkinson, Maxwell. "The Samaritans and the Elderly." *Social Science and Medicine (Oxford)* 5:483–490 (October 1971).

66. Barker, L. F. "Alleged Attempt at Suicide by a Woman of Seventy-one." *International Clinics* 3:64–67 (1930).

67. Barraclough, B. M. "Birthday Blues: The Association of Birthday with Self-inflicted Death in the Elderly." *Acta Psychiatrica Scandinavica* 54: 146–149 (August 1976).

68. Böcker, F. "Suicide in the Elderly." *Munchener Medizinische Wochenschrift* 117: 183–188 (February 7, 1975).

69. Cain, L. A. "Suicide and Attempted Suicide in Old Age." *Tijdschrift Voor Sociale Geneeskunde* 43:898–903 (1965).

70. Ciompi, L. "Psychogenic Disorders in Old Age." *Zeitschrift für Psychotherapie und Medizinische Psychologie* 16:201–211 (1966).

71. Ciompi, L. "Suicide and Suicide Attempts in Old Age." *Revue Medicale de la Suisse Romande* 86:260–262 (1966).

72. Courbon, P. & Rousset, S. "Impulsions to Suicide in an Old Epileptic Patient." *Annales Médico-Psychologuiques* 94:766–770 (1936).

73. Danneel, R. "Seasonal Differences in the Frequency of Suicide in Youth and Old Age." *Archiv fur Psychiatrie und Nervenkrankheiten (Berlin)* 221:11–13 (December 23, 1975).

74. de Alarcon, R. "Earlier Diagnosis of Depressions of the Aged." *Revista de Medicina de la Universidad de Navarra* 12:193–207 (1968).

75. de las Mata Dávila, J. S. "Discussions on Old Age and Sui-

cide." *Folia Clinica International (Barcelona)* 26:512–526 (November 1976).

76. Fedotov, D. D. et al. "Suicide Attempts in the Involutional and Aged Persons." *Zhurnal Nevropathologii i Psikhiatrii imeni S. S. Korsakova (Moscow)* 76: 406–409 (1976).

77. Gelpi, I. L. & Papexchi, A. J. "Mental Hygiene in Geriatrics: Suicide and Accidents in Old Age." *Semana Médico (Buenos Aires)* 116:1307–1312 (1960).

78. Graux, P. "Suicide of the Aged." *Lille Medical* 19:754–755 (August–September 1974).

79. Gruhle, H. W. "Suicide and Old Age." *Zeitschrift für Altersforschung* 3:21 (1941).

80. Hedri, A. 'Suicide in Advanced Age." *Schweizer Archiv für Neurologie, Neurochirurgie und Psychiatrie* 100:179–202 (1967).

81. Hedri, A. "Suicide in Old Age as a Problem of Preventative Medicine." *Therapeutische Umschau* 26:571–573 (1969).

82. Kraas, E. et al. "Suicide Attempts by Poisoning in the Aged." *Medinische Klinik (Munchen)* 66:1653–1660 (November 26, 1971).

83. Mathe, A. "Suicides of the Aged." *Vie Médicale* 48:91 (1967).

84. Modi, S. "Suicides and Old Age."*Journal of the Anthropological Society (Bombay)* 7:577–590 (1904–1907).

85. Ohara, K. "Suicide of the Aged." *Psychiatria et Neurologia Japonica* 63:1253–1268 (1961).

86. Ohara, K., Okuda, H., Tsuzura, M. & Mashino, H. "A Psychiatric Study of the Aged with Focus on Suicide." *Seishin-Igaku* 3:837–843 (1961).

87. Schaub, Hans. *Suicide and Suicide Attempts in the Elderly.* Basel: B. Schwabe, 1955.

88. Schlettwin-Gsell, D. "Self-poisoning in Older Patients." *Hippokrates* 41:297–298 (1970).

89. Seidel, K. "Inherent Dynamics of Suicide in the Elderly." *Bibliotheca Psychiatrica et Neurologica* 142:42–62 (1969).

90. Stengel, Erwin. "The Prevention of Suicide in Old Age." *Zeitschrift für Präventivmedizin* 10:474–481 (1965).

91. Taragano, Fernando. "The Psychodynamics of Day and Night Suicide in Cerebral Arteriosclerosis." *Acta Psiquiatrica y Psicologica del America Latina* 8:33–36 (1962).

92. Wiendieck, Gerd. "Social Psychologic Factors in Old Age Suicide." *Der Nervenarzt* 41:220–223 (1970).

93. Zemek, P. et al. "Some Possibilities of Prevention in Elderly People Suicide with Regard to Aid by Telephone." *Sbornik Lekarsky (Prague)* 77:308–312 (October 1975).

94. "Centenarians and Suicide." *Boston Medical and Surgical Journal* 167:142 (1912).

Related References

95. Blachly, P. H. et al. "Suicide by Physicians." *Bulletin of Suicidology* O:1–18 (December 1968).

96. Buckle, R. C., Linnane, J. & McConachy, A. "Attempted Suicide Presenting at Alfred Hospital, Melbourne." *Medical Journal of Australia* 1:754–758 (1965).

97. Burvill, P. W. "Recent Decreased Ratio of Male-Female Suicide Rates." *International Journal of Social Psychiatry* 18:137–139 (Summer 1972).

98. Cain, Albert & Fast, Irene. "The Legacy of Suicide: Observations on the Pathogenic Impact of Suicide upon Marital Partners." *Psychiatry* 29:406–411 (1966).

99. Capstick, A. "Recognition of Emotional Disturbance and the Prevention of Suicide." *British Medical Journal* 9:1179–1182 (1960).

100. Choron, Jacques. "The Psychological Autopsy." In *Suicide* New York: Scribner's, 1972, pp. 86–90.

101. Curphey, Theodore. "The Role of the Social Scientist in the Medicolegal Certification of Death from Suicide." In *The Cry For Help* (N. Farberow & E. Shneidman, eds.). New York: McGraw-Hill, 1961, pp. 110–117.

102. Dizmang, Larry & Swenson, David. *Suicide among American Indians.* DHEW Publication Number 73-9044 (HSM). Washington, D.C.: U.S. Government Printing Office, reprinted 1972.

103. Dominian, J. "Suicide as a Gesture in Marital Breakdown." In *Proceedings of the Fifth International Conference for Suicide Prevention* (Richard Fox, ed.). London, September 24–27, 1969, pp. 167–169.

104. Dublin, Louis. *Suicide: A Sociological and Statistical Study.* New York: Ronald Press, 1963.

105. Durkheim, Emile. *Suicide: A Study in Sociology.* New York: The Free Press, 1951.

106. Farber, Maurice. *Theory of Suicide.* New York: Funk & Wagnalls, 1968, pp. 16–17, 21–22, 92–93.

107. Farberow, Norman. *Taboo Topics.* New York: Atherton Press, 1963.

108. Farberow, Norman et al. "The Suicidal Patient and the Physician." *Mind* 1:69–74 (March 1963).

109. Goldberg, Martin & Mudd, Emily. "The Effects of Suicidal Behavior upon Marriage and the Family." In *Suicidal Behaviors: Diagnosis and Management* (H. L. P. Resnik, ed.). Boston: Little, Brown, 1968, pp. 348–356.

110. Graham, Ellen. "A Good Death." *The Wall Street Journal,* January 31, 1972, p. 1.

111. Hendin, Herbert. "Black Suicide." *Archives of General Psychiatry* 21:407–422 (October 1969).

112. Hendin, Herbert. *Black Suicide.* New York: Harper & Row, 1969.

113. Kahne, Merton. "Suicide Among Patients in Mental Hospitals." *Psychiatry* 31: 32–43 (February 1968).

114. Kastenbaum, Robert. "The Reluctant Therapist." In *New Thoughts on Old Age* (Robert Kastenbaum, ed.). New York: Springer, 1964, pp. 138–148.

115. Klagsbrun, Francine. *Too Young To Die: Youth and Suicide.* Boston: Houghton Mifflin, 1976.

116. Litman, Robert et al. "Investigations of Equivocal Suicide." *Journal of the American Medical Association* 184:924–929 (1963).

117. Litman, Robert. "When Patients Commit Suicide." *American Journal of Psychotherapy* 19:570–576 (1965).

118. Litman, Robert. "Acutely Suicidal Patients: Management in General Medical Practice." *California Medicine* 104:168–174 (1966).

119. Litman, Robert et al. "The Psychological Autopsy of Equivocal Deaths." In *The Psychology of Suicide* (E. Shneidman et al., eds.). New York: Science House, 1970, pp. 485–496.

120. Lowenthal, Marjorie & Haven, Clayton. "Interaction and Adaptation: Intimacy as a Critical Variable." In *Middle Age and Aging* (Bernice Neugarten, ed.). Chicago: University of Chicago Press, 1968, pp. 390–400.

121. Maris, Ronald. "The Sociology of Suicide." *Social Problems* 17:132–149 (1969).

122. Menninger, Karl. *Man Against Himself.* New York: Harcourt, Brace and World, 1938.

123. Moss, L. M. & Hamilton, D. M. "Psychotherapy of the Suicidal Patient." *American Journal of Psychiatry* 112:814–820 (1956).

124. Motto, J. A. & Greene, C. "Suicide and the Medical Community." *A.M.A. Archives of Neurology and Psychiatry* 80:776–781 (1958).

125. Neuringer, Charles. "Rigid Thinking in Suicidal Individuals." *Journal of Consulting Psychology* 28:54–58 (1964).

126. Oliven, J. F. "The Suicidal Risk: Its Diagnosis and Evaluation." *New England Journal of Medicine* 245:488–494 (September 27, 1951).

127. Parkes, C. M., Benjamin, B. & Fitzgerald, R. G. "Broken Heart: A Statistical Study of Increased Mortality Among Widowers." *British Medical Journal* 1:740–743 (1969).

128. Patel, N. S. "Pathology of Suicide." *Medicine, Science, and the Law* 13:103–109 (April 1973).

129. Poe, Elizabeth. "Suicide." *Frontier* 2:4 (August 1963).

130. Pretzel, Paul. *Understanding and Counseling the Suicidal Person*. New York: Abingdon Press, 1972.

131. Richman, Joseph & Rosenbaum, Milton. "The Family Doctor and the Suicidal Family." *Psychiatry in Medicine* 1:27–35 (1970).

132. Rockwell, Don & O'Brien, William. "Physicians' Knowledge and Attitudes about Suicide." *Journal of the American Medical Association* 225:1347–1349 (September 10, 1973).

133. Seiden, Richard. "Suicide: Preventable Death." *Public Affairs Report* (Bulletin of the Institute of Government Studies, University of California at Berkeley) 15:1–5 (August 1974).

134. Shneidman, Edwin. "You and Death." *Psychology Today* 5:78–79 (June 1971).

135. Shneidman, Edwin & Farberow, Norman. "The Logic of Suicide." In *Clues to Suicide* (E. Shneidman & N. Farberow, eds.). New York: McGraw-Hill, 1957, pp. 31–40.

136. Shneidman, Edwin & Farberow, Norman. "Sample Psychological Autopsies." In *The Psychology of Suicide* (E. Shneidman et al., eds.). New York: Science House, 1970, pp. 497–510.

137. Simon, Werner & Lumry, Gayle. "Suicide of the Spouse as a Divorce-Substitute." *Diseases of the Nervous System* 31:608–612 (September 1970).

138. Spain, David. *Post-Mortem*. New York: Doubleday, 1974, pp. 193–194, 200.

139. Swinscow, D. "Some Suicide Statistics." *British Medical Journal* 1:1417–1423 (1951).

140. Vail, D. J. "Suicide and Medical Responsibility." *American Journal of Psychiatry* 115:1006–1010 (1959).

141. Weiner, I. W. "The Effectiveness of a Suicide Prevention Program." *Mental Hygiene* 53:357–363 (1969).

142. Wolfgang, Marvin. "Suicide by Means of Victim-precipitated Homicide." *Journal of Clinical and Experimental Psychopathology* 20:335–349 (1959).

Index